C000247192

IMPLOSION

IMPLOSION

What the Internet has REALLY Done
to Culture and Communications

ANDY LAW

LONDON   MADRID
NEW YORK   MEXICO CITY
BOGOTA   BUENOS AIRES
BARCELONA   MONTERREY

PUBLISHED BY
LID Publishing Ltd.
THE LOFT, 19A FLORAL STREET
LONDON WC2E 9DS (UNITED KINGDOM)
INFO@LIDPUBLISHING.COM
LIDPUBLISHING.COM

BPR
Business Publishers Roundtable

PRINTED BY CPI GROUP (UK) LTD.

ISBN: 978-1-907794-33-9

COVER DESIGN: DAN NEVILLE
PAGE DESIGN: E-DIGITAL DESIGN LTD
ALL ILLUSTRATIONS BY DAN NEVILLE

For Tom, Livy and Venetia.
Each growing with the Net from the early days
in their own individual ways,
not thinking about it,
and sometimes sharing with me.

Thank You.

Thank You, Wayne Guthrie and Ben Little; and
Dan Neville, Jeremy Thomas, Jim Al-Khalili, Louise Dean,
Mark Pearson-Freeland, Martin Liu, Saher Sidhom, Tom
Hodgson, Tom McInnes and Zöe Kretzschmar.

*(You know how you helped, edited, added, deleted
and argued.)*

Contents

Snow

The room was suddenly rich and the great
                                    bay-window was
Spawning snow and pink roses against it
Soundlessly collateral and incompatible:
World is suddener than we fancy it.

World is crazier and more of it than we think,
Incorrigibly plural. I peel and portion
A tangerine and spit the pips and feel
The drunkenness of things being various.

And the fire flames with a bubbling sound
                                    for world
Is more spiteful and gay than one supposes—
On the tongue on the eyes on the ears in the palms
                                    of your hands—
There is more than glass between the snow
                                    and the huge roses.

                                    Louis MacNeice

1 What Happened?

It wasn't sickness, hunger or war that drove mankind to the Internet.

In 1992 there was no Necessity for it.

There was no human itch of Dissatisfaction that led industries, let alone individuals, to race for its invention.

No one asked for it.

No one predicted it.[1]

But now, 20 years later this short book needs no introduction.

---

[1] In Hamish McRae's book *The World in 2020*, published in 1994, the word "Internet" does not exist.

Because this book is about something we all know about; something as natural and common to us as the air we breathe and the water we drink.

So why write a book about the Internet? Shouldn't this be a blog at the very least? Won't this all be out of date the day after publication? Maybe. But this isn't a book about where the Internet is right now because, obviously, that will completely change tomorrow.

And it isn't a book full of prognostications about where the Internet will be in ten years time, because it doesn't really matter. We experience the Internet in real time and we'll happily go where it takes us and we'll ask painfully few questions. If it is to become "The Internet of Things"[2] (where all major physical items in our lives are digitally connected), then so be it. We'll take that development in our stride, immediately assimilate it and render it "matter-of-fact", or even mundane, in the blink of an eye. No, this is a book about us. Homo Sapiens. It's a pause for thought about what has happened to us.

Because we have changed in a substantial way and in a "there's no going back" way.

Because we have changed without asking for it or even thinking we needed to change.

Because, indisputably, we have changed with unyielding, lackadaisical, easy acceptance and we have incorporated an unbelievably powerful new element into our lives with a breathtaking level of nonchalance.

And because we have changed in a way that has added as much to the way we negotiate and transact with the

---

[2] See McKinsey for a useful description:
http://www.mckinsey.com/insights/high_tech_telecomsinternet/the_internet_of_things

world as the development of the opposable thumb did many, many millions of years ago.

We have naturally evolved and casually taken a giant step forward. The importance of the Internet in our lives has uniquely passed "down" to the very bottom of Maslow's hierarchy of needs.

Sure, many new inventions have "early adopters" who open up markets for the broader population (think of mobile phones).

But in this case, what was once a highly specialist pursuit and almost undercover skill amongst a few so called "cyber gypsies" in the mid to late '80s[3] has not become a mass-market toy, gismo, gimmick and "nice-to-have". It has become a physiological necessity for the billions who now exist online.

In 20 years the Internet has evolved from a business tool to an extension of man.

It has now become a characteristic of the normal functioning of our lives, just a tiny notch above the things without which would cause our demise: breathing, food, water and sleep, but on the same level as the physiological need for stability and sex.

No wonder that on 16th May 2011 the United Nations communiqué A/HRC/17/27 recommended that access to the Internet and mobile communication be a basic human right and that disconnecting people from the Internet was a human rights violation and against international law.

Homo Sapiens has acquired a new dependency like never before.

---

[3] See *The Cyber Gypsies* by Indra Sinha.

Our culture now depends on it.

The way we communicate totally depends on it.

And so the way we interact with all facets of the outside world has changed. As with the development of the opposable thumb, we have been given the ability to climb several more notches up the evolutionary ladder.

Maslow's Hierarchy of Needs
(incorporating the Internet)

Self-actualization

Esteem

Love/Belonging

Safety

Physiological

But something happened as we were gifted this ability. As the Internet evolved to re-shape our lives into a digital form, Homo Sapiens embraced it to furiously re-examine the analogue life that was being thrown to the wind.

This examination has been intense, ruthless, narcissistic, exciting, inventive and life-changing, all at the same time.

Let's start.

morality,
creativity,
spontaneity,
problem solving,
open mind

self-esteem, confidence,
achievement,
respect of others,
respect by others

friendship, family, sexual intimacy

security of self, employment, resources,
morality, family, health, property

stability, sex, internet,

breathing, food, water, sleep

2 First, Let's Eat.

Being on the Internet is like eating. It's something we now have to do everyday to sustain and nourish ourselves. We do it on the go; we do it on our laps; we do it on the kitchen table; we do it in the office; we do it ritualistically; we sometimes do it together; we mostly do it alone.

In wave after wave after wave across the planet, Homo Sapiens has now acquired a new bodily function:[4] Consumption of the Internet. I deliberately use the word

---

[4] It's only a matter of time before everyone on the planet is on the Internet. The latest (constantly increasing) figures from Internet World Stats shows that 34.3% of us are Internet users. Take out Africa and Asia – to give an "early adopter" snapshot – and 58.5% are consuming the Internet every single day.

"consumption" because the Internet is like eating. And I deliberately use the term "bodily function", because our Internet behaviour is as integral to our lives as respiration, ingestion, insemination, transpiration and the litany of other bodily functions that can be found in any school biology textbook.

Like eating, the Internet means different things to different people. Some eat too much, consuming hours of Web content and storing excess bytes in ever-fattening folders; bytes which are shared with friends, family and colleagues non-stop or which grow stale with non-use. Like the over consumption of anything, this can sometimes have deleterious effects.[5]

Others consume it in moderation when they need to, have to or want to. Some live in a state of permanent hunger, desperate to participate a little more but denied access because of money, geography or political control.

There are Internet gastronomists. They are tech gourmands; they love the Internet and are tuned into every aspect of its behaviour. They relish new introductions, particularly if they add spice to their existing online behaviour. These people consume sites from the everyday to the esoteric in a highly focused way.

Working closely, often symbiotically, with these gastronomists are top chefs, making their living from the Internet, working in the heat of invention, often in the

---

[5] Scientists, led by Betsy Sparrow, an Assistant Professor of Psychology at Columbia University, have shown that excessive use of the Internet affects memory: http://www.nytimes.com/2011/07/15/health/15memory.html?_r=1&

Also, *Psychology Today* reported that German scientists have discovered that Internet erotica can diminish working memory. Working memory is the ability to keep information in mind while using it to complete a task or deal with a challenge. For example, it's the capacity to juggle various bits of information as you do a math problem or keep the characters straight as you read a story. It helps you hold your goal in mind, resist distractions and inhibit impulsive choices, so it's critical to learning and planning: http://www.psychologytoday.com/blog/cupids-poisoned-arrow/201212/no-porn-better-working-memory

background. They cook up new recipes and discover new taste combinations for even greater interconnectivity. They bring us Instagram, Pinterest, Snapchat, Waze, Twitter, Omegele, Wikipedia and so on, to try out and enjoy. Many of these chefs are famous, like Larry Page and Sergey Brin of Google – celebrity chefs if you like. What they say about the Internet is important and people, markets and investors listen.

Together these two groups constitute the "Netterati" – pioneers and providers sitting atop us all defining and governing where, what and how we consume our Internet diets.

The testing of these new Internet recipes is very often down to us.

New programs are sent out in Beta-test format and served up for us to sample. We have no idea, most of the time, who the technical people behind these products actually are. We have no idea how or where they sourced the software. There is no transparency to the production of Internet software at the moment, in the way, for example, clothing or food manufacturers are obliged to reveal the entire production process and product journey.

So, often, we don't exactly know what we are consuming when we try something out on the Internet for the first time. But we still jump right in.

There are more regular cooks too, of course, serving up blogs and tweets and easy-to-understand websites.

Most of us are simply users of the Internet. Users of email and comfortable with the web sites we know.

We'll experiment a little, obviously, because we might be curious or have different predilections, in the way vegans and vegetarians choose to eat according to particular beliefs.

This newly acquired bodily function is a revolution in consumption. What cooking and dietary science has done for the performance of our bodies, now the Internet is doing for the performance of our lives.

It's the manner in which we consume the Internet that is so interesting. Just as newspapers first gathered, broadcast and ultimately elevated hearsay or tittle-tattle, now the Internet does the same for every byte of data whether it's important, unimportant, fun or frightening, silly or serious, true or untrue.

We consume with fervour and a newly honed level of impatience. We dismiss public and private time, countries and even laws to feed voraciously at will.

And it is changing us all in some fundamental ways. The change is one of increased capability learned in a haphazard and often serendipitous way. It's fun and wild and frightening and mystifying.

The opposable thumb did not change the DNA of the pre-existing environment into something completely different; it just allowed us to make greater and more inventive use of it. And, importantly, the Internet operates that way too. Internet diets are not new diets. We are just making greater and more inventive use of our pre-Internet, analogue lives.

What we consume on the Web consists of exactly the

same sort of repertoire of things we consumed before the Web took over our lives. News, views, gossip, chat, entertainment, politics, etc.

Our Analogue Life has, quite simply, just become our Digital Life.

There is no new food, if you like. There is only new "eating". It's as if every single existing store, restaurant, school, library, bar, club, cinema or theatre from around the world has been franchised and turned into a delivery service. The Internet has made the totality of our lives available outside our own front door. Open 24/7. Why wouldn't it be a feeding frenzy? It's the biggest offer on the table to Homo Sapiens since our thumbs allowed us to climb, hold and catch and put us so much higher up the food chain.

I cannot support the ambitions and arguments of those who yearn for an imagined analogue past when everything we consumed was simpler and safer and seemingly better. That's not true. While the Internet has not altered any component parts of our lives, it has fundamentally re-ordered them and served them up in a completely different way. And in any case, whilst there are numerous personal experiments, there is no going back to our analogue life. That would be pointless; and for a sustained period would, in all probability, be impossible without monumental effort and huge privations.

Like eating, the Internet has moved naturally, to infuse every single part of our daily routines.

Although we never asked for it, we now need it.

We really need it.

We categorically cannot do without it.

And so the Web has been justifiably cited as one of the greatest inventions of all time.

Now, I am not a scientist, I can't code and I am not a sociologist. Most of the people I know use more of the Internet than I do.

However, the majority of my work has been observing and advising companies large and small in many different countries. I'm on the sidelines. Only occasionally do I get into the heat of the kitchen, help build a Web-based service and so serve up something new and wonderful.

I do have a track record, though. In March 2003 I predicted a world of "enhanced inter-personal and global inter-connectivity".[6] Those words really were a mouthful. Fortunately twelve months later Facebook was launched and the term "social network" made sense of what I was trying to communicate, in just two simple words.

Pressing the pause button on an industry that moves so fast is like swimming against the tide. I nearly didn't write a single word for fear that its relevance would peak ten seconds after publication. As each day goes by something new arrives to challenge our understanding of the possibilities of the immediate future. I could cite, for example, Corning's Willow Glass technology. But what's the point? It will surely be old by the time this publication is available online.

But that is the point; pressing the pause button allows for some reflection. I cite at the beginning Louis MacNeice's

[6] *Experiment At Work*, 2003.

exquisite short poem Snow because of its observation of a world that can be naturally crazy and "more of it than we think".

The Internet has at its heart a sense of there being more of it than we think. MacNeice talks in the poem of "The drunkenness of things being various". The Internet is providing a giddying ride at the moment not least for retailers. The sudden absence of fixed High Street landmarks such as Borders, Circuit City and Woolworths takes you and me on their giddying ride, throwing us into the arms of competitors on and offline, some of whom we have heard of and others whose (often kooky) names pop up in an instant.

Observing the Internet is not easy. If you Google "Internet", you can choose from 7 billion results. That's one for every person on the planet. And why not? This is a universal bodily function and therefore just about every single person has a justifiable claim on the Internet, or will have within a very short period of time. If you Google "Web", you'll be met with 16 billion places to visit (and less than 15% of them will have anything to do with spiders). [7]

You have to stand outside of the Internet in a curious unreal world to observe whether the Internet is, in fact, something we now blindly, slavishly and routinely consume, given its 100% pervasiveness. And if so, the big question for me is how it has altered my outlook on life, in the way that the development of food production and the rituals of eating have anchored so much of my daily life.

I understand the value of the things that reside firmly at the lower end of Maslow's hierarchy of needs. I have the same physiological needs that all of us have. I do

---

[7] If you Google "God", a mere 1.6 billion results appear, but connecting these points spins the book into an altogether different direction.

not need the Internet to help me sleep, for example. I have the same requirement for personal safety and job security that most people I know need. But I recognize that it has secured a place, if not at the absolute base of Maslow's hierarchy, then surely just one step up.

The Internet is enabling many of the things that I now feel need to be brought to me faster. If they are brought to me at a lower price, that is a bonus – but not always a requirement.

It is so important to us that it is making some people fixated on certain aspects of it; conspiracy sites, privacy issues, non-stop tweeting, for example.

Internet addiction is a natural by-product of Internet consumption.

So has it altered the way I view my existence? Many inventions, like the axel and wheel, printing, radio and television, have certainly enabled me to alter my outlook on life. They have taken me to new people and places.

The obvious answer is "Yes". I now share the same physiological need for the Internet that everyone else does. I check my emails and messages as soon as I wake up. Importantly I do this with much more verve and anticipation than I do waiting for letters to drop through the letter-box. I often realize that I have been on the Internet for much longer than I'd thought, meandering through a wonderful, labyrinthine net of passageways and doorways – often ending up somewhere unexpected and then alerting my friends to my discovery.

Any question that pops into my head or arises in

discussion is answered in a nano-second. My life is being captured in an orderly place-and-time driven way (through Facebook) that would have been practically impossible to manage in our analogue past.

The thought of not having the Internet makes me feel that a fundamental part of how I operate has been disabled. While anyone of 30 years age or younger may justifiably claim to have never been without it, even people who conducted a perfectly ordinary existence without it now claim that they could not do without it.[8]

---

[8] For example, two-thirds of the UK's over-65s say they could not live without the Internet, according to new research commissioned by Plusnet. http://www.cable.co.uk/news/plusnet-finds-63-of-over-65s-cant-live-without-the-internet-801575336/

3 Now it's Time for a Coffee.

A coffee pot was an early image on the Internet. Now little, everyday things – like coffee pots – are becoming the stuff of the Web. We are being driven relentlessly to what we already know by a contrary, counter-intuitive force.

First, I need a cup of coffee.

Not a fresh one. An old one. One from the pot in the Trojan Room at Cambridge University that was the very first thing I saw online some time in the Spring of 1992.

I was in Los Angeles attending a routine management meeting at the cooler-than-cool ad agency Chiat/ Day. The Head of IT, Stevan ("Steve") Alburty, was enthusiastically demonstrating to a small group of us something called the World Wide Web. Eight or nine of us crowded round the small colour screen of a soon-to-be-obsolete Mac II, jostling for position, joshing, joking and craning our necks to see what all the fuss was about. We were giggling about how "experienced professionals" could get so excited about a glorified electronic word processor. "Excited" didn't even scratch the surface of how insanely pre-occupied Steve was. He teased us and raised our expectation levels. "Typical Steve, always something new-fangled up his sleeve."

We knew about the Internet. We had already been utilizing its commercial communication benefits for well over two years, linking our offices around the world via Quickmail, Apple's early email system with its own unique protocol; but, Steve explained, after snapping us to attention, the new World Wide Web opened up the Internet way beyond email and offered us something much more expansive via a different access system called hypertext transfer protocol (http).

He pressed a button and stood back. "Take a look," he intoned.

We did what we were told and stared at the screen and after much flickering a black and white image of a coffee pot was noticeably observed to be scrolling down the screen. We waited. Another image. Same pot, less coffee. More flickering. More waiting. After a while we could see that the pot had been lifted off its stand by an unknown hand. Steve remarked that the unknown hand had no idea we were watching it perform. We felt a little odd about that. Soon, a cup of coffee was poured. This was live computing. This wasn't broadcasting. This was personal, micro observation and the fact that the coffee pot was some 5,500 miles away had not escaped our notice.

We gasped.

It was a great cup of coffee. It was a very strong cup of coffee.

It was so strong it sent our heads spinning; we were heady; we were mesmerized by it.

You see, I need that cup of coffee to place-mark a divide between my analogue and digital lives; and you need it as a virtual caffeine kick-start to remind yourself of your first engagement with the Web. Take a moment to remember it.

Have you remembered? Maybe you can't, because your first engagement with the Web was as natural as taking your first steps when you were just a toddler. And let's be honest who can remember that?

If you can remember it (and most of you should), then good! Remember it as the moment something completely unexpected and life changing and ubiquitous and culturally contrary was ushered into our world.

Culturally contrary?

Don't get me wrong, "culturally contrary" is not negative; clearly we are uniquely privileged to be living and witnessing the unfolding of a true and wonderful technological break through. Tim Berners-Lee, by opening up the Internet to everyone via http, is an inventor every bit as important and influential as Michael Faraday, Thomas Edison or Alexander Graham Bell, for example.

But we don't need to get into how large and pervasive and wonderful the Internet is. Again, we all know this. It's like asking how big "air" is. And we don't need data to tell us. We know it instinctively. After all, we don't ask ourselves, or measure, how we walk or talk; it is just a natural daily, automatic part of what makes us the kind of animals we are.

We need to get into something else. You see nobody, not even Tim Berners-Lee and his team at CERN, had any real idea of the consequences of what they had ushered in. How could they? It would be at least a decade, maybe two, before the realization could strike home.

The Internet is contrary. It is the opposite of previous cultural innovations. It does not behave like the prestigious scientific inventions that have preceded it, or like the anthropological step changes that now define us, such as the arrival of human language, for example.

It has a stronger reverse polarity coupled with a much greater magnetism than its eminent precursors lined up over our long history of human evolution.

When we all first saw the coffee pot pour its first cup of coffee, we all inhaled an extra large gasp of air.

We are still inhaling.

Because just when we think it is time to draw breathe, another extraordinary Web development occurs.

The Internet is behaving in a way that is affecting everything we do. And it is making us think about things in a way we have never previously thought. Importantly, however, it is a different pioneering force than that we felt it might have been when we first started imagining its possibilities.

As a discovery the Web is useful, interesting and often delightful. But it is also disconcerting to many. Worrying to some. Frightening to others.

And not because of the fact that it exists per se, but because of what it has been doing since it arrived.

That Cambridge coffee pot lit a fuse at the end of a very unusual and profoundly different stick of "innovation dynamite". Every Chairman, CEO, marketer, brand-custodian, product manager, family, student, parent, pensioner, revolutionary and you-name-it has felt, possibly just for a nano-second, that "something else is going on".

The initial detonation of energy that ensued throughout the '90s has created a revised digital global culture that has grown to become institutionally comfortable and disconcerted at the same time and which poses new threats and opportunities in equal measure to almost every aspect of our lives.

A type of detonation is the right way to talk about the effect of the Internet on the way we live, work and communicate.

Not just because it describes our accelerated online and offline journeys and the new places we find ourselves propelled into (for example, new relationships, conversations, groups, countries, retail outlets, data sources, homes and so on), but also because its shock waves have forced so much of our daily activity into a completely new direction.

It has displaced and disintermediated our well-ordered media, in a rude and ruthless way, and created a new order of interconnectedness that is as creative as it is confusing.

It has re-worked our living space and our inter-personal relationships.

It has ushered in new entertainment in new forms from new places, blurring what is important, unimportant, real and unreal.

It has both raised and demolished new hopes and ideals for new political agendas across the globe.

It has let new genres of spirituality flourish and fly on the virtual breezes of popular opinion. This spirituality is most often personal rather than public and is accelerating the decline of some organized, community based religions.

It has abolished media apartheid, so that fringe subcultures, ideas and products can now move with less restriction into the mainstream.

It has demanded an overturning of all the major propositions of modern marketing communications.

It has, to date, made the planet more Asian, shifting

closely held notions of where the growing centres of commercial and academic excellence are now coming from.

And it has added new dimensions to the concept of "discovery" as seeking to know more about what and whom we already know is now just as valid (if not, more valid) as discovering new things.

We are witnessing a total inversion of Invention. Whereas cultural milestones have been created through the invention of new ideas which themselves drive on to spawn even more dramatic developments, the Web has not, to date, done this.

Just as fast as it takes us to new places and new thinking, it draws us back to a greater and more intense and faster realization of what we have already invented.

Allow yourself the briefest and scantiest of trips down Cultural Evolution's Memory Lane. [9]

---

[9] To avoid filling an entire book, I have made a personal selection of just those cultural evolutionary points that represent certain milestones – biasing them towards communication leaps.

The FOXP2 Gene permitting Human Speech (c. 200,000BC),

The Evolution of Language (c. 150,000BC),

The Invention of Boats (at least 130,000BC),

Formal Religion (c. 50,000BC),

Cave Paintings (c. 30,000BC),

Counting (c. 8,000BC),

Writing (c. 5,000BC),

The Domestication of the Horse (c. 4,000BC),

The Formation of Cities (c. 4,000BC),

The Axel and Wheel (c. 3,500BC),

Complex Mathematics (c. 3,000BC),

The Paved Road (c. 2,500BC),

Papyrus Writing (c. 2,400BC),

Organized Warfare (c. 2,300BC),

Sophisticated Weapons and Tools (c. 1,250BC),

Planned, Controlled and Managed Empire (c. 27BC),

Woodblock Printing (c. 220),

The Printing Press (c. 1440),

Newspapers (c. 1609),

Commercial Steam Power (c. 1712),

Lithography and Billboards (c. 1793),

The Telegraph (c. 1837),

The Telephone (c. 1876),

Commercial Electricity (c. 1880),

The Automobile (c. 1885),

Radio (c. 1895),

Cinema (c. 1895),

The Airplane (c. 1905),

The TV (c. 1927),

Reprogrammable Computers (1948),

Satellites (1957) and

Space Travel (1961).

All these confidently stand as major examples of landmark evolutionary developments, which in their own way accelerated three important components of our human story.

1. The progression of human communication.

2. The expansion of discovery.

3. The growth of global culture.

Each of these evolutionary developments progressed the possibilities of human exploration and expanded the cultural horizons of the communities that benefitted from them. In many cases advanced evolutionary change, like the domestication of the horse, defined the cultures that embraced the opportunities they were given. With the taming of the horse for travel, communities became aware that they could garner greater safety and nourishment beyond their own small worlds. Humans mounted horses to see, seize and secure more of the assets that would make their own communities safer and stronger. Men became Horsemen.

Such seismic cultural maturation points exploded and drove out, worldwide, pioneering symbiotic developments accelerating intellectual, philosophical, commercial and technical human expansion. So it was that the seemingly straightforward achievement of the building and development of roads, for example, led eventually to super highways, which in turn led to settlers creating new spaces and, of course, new opportunities for themselves and others. Often the virility of such inventions creates an explosive ripple effect for generations.

Although the earliest examples of the paved road stretch back over 4,500 years, the Trans-Continental Highway last century and the Western Europe-Western China Trans-Continental Highway this century are pure examples of this ripple effect. Strings of smaller ribbon developments, coupled with a larger variety of tradable goods have and will create tangible, measurable, change.

Take a closer look at the latter of these two Highways. The total length of the Western Europe-Western China Trans-Continental Highway is almost 8,445 kilometres. The project is a huge investment (costs are around $5.5 billion) but it's a valid investment because its completion will shorten the time of delivery of goods from China to Europe (and vice versa) by almost four times, compared to current methods of sea transport.[10]

We can expect to see an explosion of new, even unseen, Chinese and Asian goods flooding into Western Europe armed with their highly effective weapon – economic advantage. Goods from Western Europe to China now too have their new channel forged. These goods will settle into new communities, which in turn will adopt and adapt them and, very quickly, they will find them commonplace.

Each evolutionary development had its own "super-effects", building and moulding new cultural identities and, yes, demolishing and re-shaping others.

These were explosive developments. They emitted a power that created societal shockwaves. They carried, with immense force and with an enormous number of related ideas, an energy of obvious and, in the main, positive change. Reaching out to discover "the new"

---

[10] Currently, transporting goods from China to Europe takes between 15 and 45 days through the Suez Canal by sea or via the TransSib road.

led to a progression over time of new thinking and the learning of new cultures and languages. Processing "the new" took the time it took. Sometimes years, often centuries.

The Internet, allowing for a rapid development of new applications and features, has also created a shock wave. But it is a shockwave with a difference.

The Internet is spreading by itself. At no point did we humans ever climb a mountain or cross an ocean to discover it. It comes to us and never asks what we want or why we may want it. Instead of carrying culture out into new places it has a strong dynamic that carries all it can find and transports it back inwards with an in-built assumption that we want it, need it and will love it.

Everything is effortlessly brought to us, right into our homes and phones, offices and schools. It is a shock wave that snaps us back into the world we already know and forcefully insists that we re-examine how we are already living.

It is taking us back into ourselves and exploding inwards the behaviours we already know.

We are filling our minds daily with things we didn't set out to discover and with things we already knew.

It's exciting. We are devouring things because we can, not because we feel we need them. We are filling our minds, "all of a sudden" and to our personal satisfaction, through a source that has no end game and makes no demands.

That's what I mean by "culturally contrary".

This landmark creation, the most significant for many, many generations, impels us into whatever version of "the extant world" is created at any one moment in time.

It is now possible to see that the symbolic coffee pot detonated something highly unusual.

The Web is not, like its worthy innovations before it, an explosion.

It is an implosive force.

It is annihilating and creating simultaneously. It is creating a typhoon of noise that distorts the voices of previous tradition and order. It is moving at breakneck speed. It is picking up the signs, symbols, memes and modus operandi of modern life and dropping them all, breaking them and watching them melt and meld together in an intense heat of activity, creating new products and ideas, which themselves fall victim to the implosion within which they were created. So MySpace comes. And goes. And comes back again. And…?

If it all sounds dizzy, that's because it is. It's been the biggest ride for over 20 years.

It's time for another cup of coffee.

One I can smell.

And drink.

THE
MEDIUM
IS
THE
MESS

4 The Medium is the Mess.

The World Wide Web has displaced and deconstructed our well-ordered media, in a rude and ruthless way, and created a new order of interconnectedness that is as confusing as it is creative.

Here are Two Media Tales that can never happen again.

On 30th October 1938 the American actor, director, writer and producer Orson Welles famously dramatized a Martian invasion of Earth. His source material, which he adapted with some artistic licence, was the British author H.G. Wells' 1897 science fiction novel *War of the Worlds*. Wells and his "Mercury Theatre on the Air" actors repurposed the story and broadcast it. It was so well done that to the listener it appeared to be a genuine news broadcast story about an unexplained object landing at Grovers Mill, New Jersey. The broadcast, as we all know, resulted in considerable real-life chaos on the streets.

Practical joking aside, it was a fascinating extension of a fascinating medium, blurring fact and fiction with considerable panache.

During that same year H.G. Wells himself gave a series of lectures to various eminent scientific groups. He published these lectures under the title *World Brain*.

Wells had enthusiastically embraced Radio as an invention full of potential and real value to mankind and he was delighted that Orson chose to bring together his much-loved book, with his much-loved medium. (Two years later, in 1940, the two men would meet in a radio station in San Antonio, Texas and amongst other things H.G. Wells declared how excited he was about Orson's upcoming innovation, a new motion picture called *Citizen Kane*, using previously untried techniques.)

In his lectures of 1938 Wells predicted that one day every home in the world would own a radio and so could listen without bias, prejudice or censorship to free thinking and, more importantly, free talking commentators. (Such was the belief in the BBC.)

But his imagination took him further. He predicted this

explosion of the medium of radio would engender new ideas and promulgate new technology.

He predicted that one day radios would not only receive transmissions, they would send out transmissions as well, from each home to any other home willing to tune in and listen.

In his future vision radios would facilitate a global and rapid broadcast and reception of transmissions from individual radio to individual radio.

He develops this thinking and says that he predicts a stratosphere emerging of interlinked messaging, a "net", he thought, which, usefully (given the year in which he was espousing these views) would alert the world to despots.

Again, Wells went further. He suggested that because this stratosphere, or "net", contained such singular and uncontaminated output (from each individual radio) it would eventually house All Knowledge. In fact, all the knowledge that anyone could ever have wanted.

He called the aggregation of this knowledge, World Encyclopaedia.

As a prediction of not only the Internet (and more specifically Wikipedia) but also our general state of interconnectedness, Wells' *World Brain* essays are astonishingly prescient. But more interestingly as a ray of hope for positive and helpful inter-human communication, such prescience is formidable, to say the least.

The famous Orson Welles 30th October broadcast was

also an unintended demonstration of the power of radio to influence a mass audience. It was "broadcast messaging" that could not be immediately challenged.

But that particular brand of mass marketing was in fact already well understood by, amongst others, the National Socialist Party, which in 1938 was the governing party in Germany. The Nazi communication machine, led by their Head of Propaganda Josef Goebbels, made radio their medium in a way that no one else had before or has since.[11]

H.G. Wells had been concerned, nervous and somewhat mesmerized by the rise of the Nazis. He naively and optimistically saw an intertwined network of radios as an early warning system and a cumulative knowledge base without recognizing that the medium can be used and manipulated by both sides of any "argument".

As it transpired radio played a highly integrated role in World War Two and it went on to become the primary civilian link to contemporaneous news and entertainment through the '40s and '50s.[12]

As an interesting postscript to the way the Nazis used radio, in the 1940 San Antonio radio broadcast Messrs Welles and Wells remark on how Hitler had used Orson's *War of the Worlds* broadcast to explain that the panic that ensued was a fine example of the decadence of democracies.

Radio stepped aside from its primary communication position at 1.40 pm EST on 22nd November 1963 when

---

[11] The Japanese also made a good but limited use of radio as a propaganda machine, inflicting Tokyo Rose on the ears of the mainly US forces fighting in the Pacific.

[12] Orson's 1938 broadcast was the first but not the only time a dramatized news story of H.G. Wells' *War of the Worlds* was mistaken for an account of real events. In November 1944 the play caused a similar panic when it was broadcast in Santiago, Chile. Media was not global and was not connected, so it was easy to conjure up the same trick again in February 1949. This time it was performed by a radio station in Quito, Ecuador, provoking an angry mob to surround the radio station and, in fact, burn it to the ground.

TV's announcement and continuous live coverage and story-telling of the highly visual assassination of John F. Kennedy, (followed swiftly by the on air assassination of Lee Harvey Oswald) swept TV into pole position and relegated radio to the role of secondary, or support, medium.

Less than three months later TV was to enshrine its dominance.

At 8.00pm EST, on Sunday 9th February 1964, The Beatles appeared live on the *Ed Sullivan* TV show. An estimated 78 million people watched. The show had been presaged by a deluge of news items reporting the arrival of The Fab Four. The show was not broadcast live around the world. That was not possible.[13] You had to be there, in the United States, to watch it. 78 million US viewers was a big figure, representing approximately 38% of all TV homes in the USA.

If you weren't in the United States on that day, or indeed, if you weren't ever going to be anywhere The Beatles were likely to be, you had to wait a long three years to be able to see John, Paul, George and Ringo perform for you while they were thousands of miles away in another country. Such was the march of technology that it was now possible for you to enjoy them from the vantage point of your own sofa in your own country. And for the first time you would be joined by many other different people from many other different countries. And all at the same time.

Now watched by an estimated 400 million people in 26

---

[13] The Telstar 1 satellite, which became the world's first active communications satellite, launched on 10th July 1961 from Cape Canaveral, Florida. Two days later it made history by transmitting the first television test signal from the Andover Earth Station in Maine to the Pleumeur-Bodou Telecom Center in Brittany, France. This test, featuring JFK, presaged the global live link of five years later, which featured artists such as Maria Callas and Pablo Picasso representing their different nations. The Beatles closed the show.

countries, the first global live TV program was broadcast via satellite on 25th June 1967. It closed with a simple message. It was The Beatles singing *All You Need Is Love*.

Only two years later, at 02:56 UTC, on the 21st July 1969, 530 million people watched the first humans ever to walk on the surface of the moon. This constituted around 14% of the total population of the world at the time.

Again, a simple message was transmitted to the world. "That's one small step for [a] man, one giant leap for mankind."

Along with increasingly reported and repeated global news, these explosive events, brought to us by the phenomenal coupling of two wonderful inventions, TV and Satellites, ushered in something new.

Global cultural homogeneity. That is to say, we started getting used to seeing ourselves objectively as global citizens, sharing opinions and ideas simultaneously on a wide spectrum of globally transmitted subjects.

It is not too fanciful to say that "Earthrise", the name given to William Anders 1968 photograph of the Earth rising over the moon, is the one image that crystallized this emergent global, homogenous consciousness.

Earthrise helped us visualize one simple and now hotly contested concept – globalization – and in turn activated hundreds of businesses, protests, products and movements keen to demonstrate its benefits and its dangers, be they environmental, philosophical, social or commercial.

The astronaut Buzz Aldrin summed it up for me once

when I asked him one evening what it was like to see the Earth from the Moon.

He said it was sheer beauty. It was like the most beautiful but fragile silver blue Christmas tree ornament hanging in as black a black void as you could possibly get. He came close and looked me straight in the eyes and with real purpose said that as soon as he saw Earth hanging there, still and silent and so, so delicate, he just wanted to go back immediately and understand it, protect it and, he guessed, save it.

Those 1960s TV audience figures pale into insignificance against the claimed billions who watch global events in the 21st century such as Olympic Opening Ceremonies.

And now the Internet scoops up billions of people effortlessly every single day.

In fact, getting a big audience today isn't a big story, because those figures for global TV events positively vaporize against Internet audience figures. Consider the gargantuan fact that YouTube's Content ID system scans over 100 years of video every day and that over 500 years of YouTube video are watched every day on Facebook. Three billion hours of video are watched every month on YouTube. By the way, that's just this year's figures.[14]

And anyone, wherever, whenever, can watch exactly the same footage, although, in a distinctly different way from the global satellite broadcasts, the viewing experience is not so much shared as shareable.

It's a personal experience.

Google bought YouTube in October 2006 and its 2012

[14] http://www.youtube.com/t/press_statistics/

new product offerings are designed to do one thing. Attract more massive global audiences by facilitating more attractive content.

More attractive content provides more ad revenues and now Google receives around $1.5 billion from YouTube. Forecasters expect that to increase to $15 billion by 2020. [15]

A coupling such as Google and YouTube has been a part of the re-framing of conventional TV channels. In an implosive drive the previous global media homogeneity is breaking up and being replaced by fractal, bit part, one-on-one viewing.

This is not the end of TV as so many commentators love to proclaim. Far from it. [16]

In fact, television viewing has never been higher in the US, Europe and UK. The increase in viewing comes from all demographic groups and all ages. Since 2007, average television viewing has increased by over 20% – the highest figures on record, and, pointedly, a record rate of growth. [17]

On-Demand, or "time-shifted" viewing (recording your favourite shows, requesting movies and shows online, etc) has helped keep these viewing figures high. It's this that the "Death-Of-TV" pundits forget. It is still TV. It's just that we are consuming it differently.

And watching live TV is also still a major part of our chosen entertainment. Deloitte's 2010 Media Democracy Survey revealed that 83% of French, 74% of UK, 73% of Brazilian, 71% of Japanese, 69% of German, 61% of Canadian

[15] *Forbes.* http://www.forbes.com/sites/greatspeculations/2013/01/23/google-earnings-ad-revenues-jump-helped-by-mobile-push/

[16] A recent example is Stephen Totilo:
http://kotaku.com/the-coming-death-of-the-television-476947234

[17] D. Brennan, "TVs Not Dead", *Market Leader* magazine, June 2013.

and 57% of US viewers claimed to prefer watching their favourite TV shows live. Inevitably these figures will decline as we adjust to the possibilities of consuming broadcast material in different places at different times.

The fractal break up of TV is a prelude to a completely different way of consuming the content we have all loved for so many years. Remember, there is no new "food". Only new "eating".

An example of "new eating" can be seen in the increase in binge-viewing of boxed sets, or series dramas, such that entire seasons of multi-part dramas, like Netflix's *House of Cards*, or *The West Wing* or *Lost* are consumed by people in a single weekend.

Internet-enabled smart TVs allow us not to worry about what is being broadcast; just as long as we know we are able to consume anything that has been broadcast.

That's different, unexpected and good.

In fact we now know that we can watch almost anything that has been, is being, or will in the future be broadcast by any individual or organization.

This is not broadcasting. It isn't even "narrowcasting". It is personally selected "me-casting", feeding our understanding of our own needs and desires. I don't need to worry how many channels I have. I have to worry about thinking what I want to watch. Once, TV editors told me what to watch; now I must edit or delete the universe of broadcasting myself.

Although supportive data is thrown around by many different, but interested, parties, we don't need statistics to tell us that we are at the beginning of the decline of conventional (analogue, if you like) broadcast TV.[18] It's a decline that neither the TV sets nor the satellites that brought you All You Need Is Love had anything to do with it. They were technological vehicles on a journey outward, carrying new people and ideas to newer people and places. Instinctively, genetically, if you like, audiences were compelled to pursue that self-same urge.

Analogue TV's decline is not a result of one explosive cultural innovation naturally transmogrifying into something else in the way the telegraph, for example, came to become the telephone.

TV broadcast's fragmented and directional journey of demise is due to a reversal of the laws of innovation. A new implosive force had been created in CERN and its earliest trophy victim will have been conventional fixed-time TV broadcasting.

For a pot-shot at conventional TVs point of no return, the Diffusion Group (TDG) plots the summer of 2019 as the moment at which Internet Video takes over from Live Broadcast TV. But even as I look at the date 2019 and marry it to the growth rate of time-shift TV and online newcomers, I feel compelled to argue it will be sooner. We are seeing Intel announcing a Pay TV service and Amazon releasing a television set-top box that would stream video over the Internet into customers' homes; we are witnessing the sophisticated development of YouTube and Netflix and we are enjoying the power and flexibility of Video On Demand.

That's how it's working now. Faster and furiously.

---

[18] Ok then. In May 2012 The Nielsen Company, which takes TV set ownership into account when it produces ratings, reported that 96.7% of American households now own sets, down from 98.9% previously. It's the beginning.

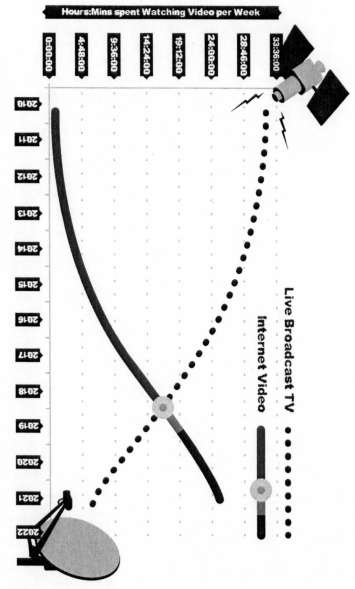

Hours:Mins spent Watching Video per Week

Live Broadcast TV

Internet Video

Source: The Diffusion Group (TDG), 2012

Just as content consumption is evolving, the TV sets themselves, of course, have also evolved neatly into a smarter animal. The original creative explosion of early TV technology has bent to the new demands of the Internet. Briefly, TVs and computers flirted and produced smart monitors. Now TVs are a whole new breed with an intelligence to understand your total viewing requirements and nuances – things that even you yourself may often forget are now served to you courteously and with ease and fluidity.

Smart TVs look as closely into you, your life and habits as it is possible to do without you being physically invaded. They narrow down to who you are and what you like. They also judiciously allow for any randomness or promiscuity that you might let in to your entertainment life. An excessive and increasing mountain of online content harnessed to smart (and progressively smarter) TVs are wired to understand how you and I are wired. They employ on screen guides to help take us to the channels that will most excite us, based on algorithms of inputted, or previous, behavior. And they encourage us to edit or adapt our viewing so they can offer even smarter viewing suggestions.

I look into the grey-black screen of my TV monitor and what I am essentially looking at is an image of my "broadcast self".

It's definitely alluring and makes for hyper-personalized TV.

In fact, everything that I like on TV has come to me with me hardly making a move.

It's powerful, implosive and curiously narcissistic.

The reason that those two earlier media stories cannot happen again is that the most important product of the Orson Welles broadcast and the Beatles/Neil Armstrong events were not, at the time, the numbers. It was the cultural impact. The shared wonder.

Today we know the numbers. We know the wonder of the numbers. We know the years, the months, days and minutes of things. We have access to minutiae, because minutiae have come to us. We list and sort. We are able to dig deeper and deeper into events of the past, both ours and those of other people. We know, for example, that on the 8th of February 1964, George Harrison had tonsillitis and missed the *Ed Sullivan Show* rehearsal. If we wanted, we could almost certainly find out the brand name of the medicines he took at the time. And the specific drugstore they came from. And the name of the assistant who dispensed them. And where he or she is living, or not, today. And what their house looks like. We could link up and ask questions: "Did you meet George Harrison, or was an aide sent?" We could know how many children and grandchildren the assistant has and where they go on vacation.

This is "internalized discovery". It is the highly energetic pursuit of more and more to the tiniest point of no return. It is tunneling down and digging deeper.

This is an effect of implosion. Where data is used not to reach outwards but to peer inwards and discover the things we didn't know about or the things we had briefly heard about.

In the 1960s those cultural impacts were uniquely TV impacts. They were analyzed and debated at the time as one impact. All the limited channels of media that were available at that time were open to expand upon exemplar TV events such as these.

Today these events would be discussed and debated alongside a plethora of other instantly accessible cultural events. But importantly, of course, TV is very unlikely to be the primary source. The explosion of devices that carry Web content provides instant data to consider, or even counteract, widely held, shared beliefs. The Beatles appearance on the *Ed Sullivan Show*, if, hypothetically, shown today would be subject to comparison of other simultaneous news stories. Such as Katy Perry's 37 million Twitter followers,[19] which in turn lags behind Lady Gaga's 38 million;[20] who is some way behind Justin Bieber's 40 million.[21] Whatever is trending on Twitter regularly makes it into the headlines, which, without the blink of an eye, are then accessed via a multitude of platforms.

The explosion of media since the arrival of the telephone, radio, cinema and TV over 100 years ago has itself caused an incessant ripple of cultural explosions across a wide spectrum of our commercial and recreational lives.

The Ed Sullivan Show conferred upon The Beatles what the remarkable sociologist/anthropologist Pierre Bourdieu called "Symbolic Capital". [22] To Bourdieu, writing in 1979, professionals who live on the sale of cultural services (for example, Rock Stars, Artists, Writers) are successful on the equal accumulation of four forms of capital: Economic (Wealth); Social (Network); Cultural (Zeitgeist); and Symbolic (Fame).

The Ed Sullivan Show, a product of the medium of TV, re-capitalized The Beatles and projected them into a

---

[19] 37,695,983 by June 2013.

[20] 38,126,604 by June 2013.

[21] 40,273,287 by June 2013.

[22] Pierre Bourdieu, *Distinction: A Social Critique of the Judgement of Taste.*

totally new cultural universe, way beyond the streets of Hamburg and Liverpool. Faster than we often like to recall, The Beatles sped effortlessly through acoustic and visual innovation, through fashion, drugs, sex and class disruption to culturally defining acts of joy and defiance. In less than seven years, they had advanced many strata of global culture in a way that previously it may have taken 70 years.

However, by selling 176,000 copies of *Up All Night*, the British pop group One Direction secured the top spot on the US Billboard charts with their debut and changed everything. They had achieved what The Beatles never achieved – and they did it in less than seven months.

Bourdieu's model is itself adapting as it breaks and mutates in the implosive effects of the Web and the sociologist's prediction model is having to embrace Andy Warhol's less scientific, but eerily prescient, 1968 observation that "in the future, everyone will be world-famous for 15 minutes".

What Bourdieu might have thought took some time to achieve now can take no time at all. The Internet has modified his model because of the speed of networking opportunities.

Being Social (Social Network sites neatly parcel up one part of Bourdieu's model) is easier than ever, but doesn't alter the fact that for sustained success you still require the other three forms of capital.

The Web can network you. It can make you money and it can provide a platform for doing or saying something new and intriguing right now. It offers a ready-to-go fame kit and can therefore make anyone rich and famous if only for a brief moment.

And of course there will be many more "firsts" like One Direction. In an implosive cultural environment, as we shall see in more detail in Chapter 7, matter (data, people, achievements, etc) speeds up, fragments and gets smaller. Implosions create a multitude of small things. And, of course, each "small thing" has its own validity. The problem is that a world of a billion valid things creates a fog of discovery, obscuring potentially genuine beacons of explosive thinking.

The result of fractal media for the music entertainment industry is an accelerating chaos of fragmented bands and musicians, viewed, sampled and deleted through an accelerating spectrum of devices (increasingly mobile devices[23]) with each parvenu entrant sifting ideas from their predecessor, asserting their contemporary importance and blurring the previously explicit value of other co-existing artists.

It offers for the first time something very unique. Individuals can plunder the myriad artistic offers and, in an inversion of the "fan" model, where the power lies with the artist, can exert high levels of influence. Aggregated blogs, such as Universal Wax, are now beginning to call artists to attend the screens of individuals. Not the other way round.

There is a proliferation of bands and musicians, because they represent the many small differences in taste and predilection of the public at large. They are pure and real ingredients of our web consumption and offer genuine quality and diversity.

[23] In 2011, *Strategy Analytics* cited 108 billion mobile videos viewed worldwide; in 2012 that number has already climbed to 280 billion views.

Broadcast TV has been broken up by this implosion and this has had a disruptive effect on conventional advertising.

Advertising is atomized across all forms of content, including DIY YouTube content and search engine information. It is now stretching itself to cover all viewing possibilities of all audiences. Now, when you search for something on the Internet you are being advertised to by the company that has paid the most to get a high Google ranking. Communication has rapidly moved from sedate and seductive to brisk and bite-sized. As more devices and more websites appear, the amount of content to travel through is increasing. Vast "distances" of subject matter can be covered with proprietary social media organizers and website managers.

Of course there still remain 24 hours in a day, and the simple equation Speed = Distance/Time demonstrates what happens when you surf more Web content in the same period of time.

Things speed up.

No wonder everybody at some point (including children) makes the observation: "I'm sure life is running faster than it used to."

When things speed up, your vision of other things blur.

There is a blurring of content, an over supply of channels and an array of devices on which to view anything. Simultaneous use ("second screening") of more than one device is now commonplace across the globe (see Nielsen charts overleaf).

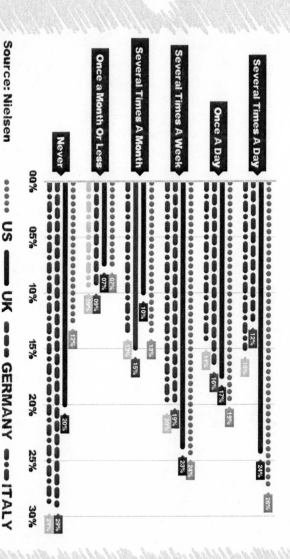

Simultaneous use of Tablet while watching TV

Source: Nielsen

····· US —— UK ●●● GERMANY ●●● ITALY

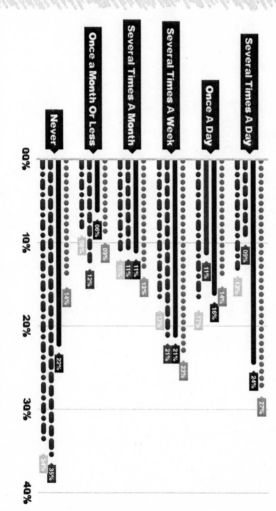

Simultaneous use of Smartphone while watching TV

Source: Nielsen

•••• US ⎯⎯ UK ••• GERMANY ••• ITALY

Several Times A Day
09%
13%
24%
27%

Once A Day
11%
14%
16%
17%

Several Times A Week
17%
21%
21%
23%

Several Times A Month
11%
11%
12%
13%

Once a Month Or Less
06%
08%
09%
12%
14%

Never
22%
34%
35%

What was global and shared is now personal and shareable.

TV's role as the global voice of incident and entertainment has now been atomized and edited to such a degree that it is difficult to make the claim that it retains the premier status it held as it reported the unfolding news of JFK's assassination.

Alert messaging and personally selected information grabs are now the go-to places for instant news.

There is no longer a broadcast voice. There are millions of voices. And they are all talking at the same time to and at each other.

All media consumption has been doubling every 25 years since 1900. And until someone finds more hours in the day, this increase will lead to rapid blurring and fragmentation. Ultimately this in turn leads to the inconsequential nature of anything broadcast and the importance of self-selection.

If it is the summer of 2019 that finally bids sayonara to conventional broadcast TV, look what happens in 2020.

The chart opposite shows the World Association looking forward back in 2008.

Five years ago, 50% of all global media was digital. By 2020 that ratio will be 80%.

Almost all media, print, TV, radio and outdoor, will undergo implosive change making any consistency of communication almost impossible.[24]

My two media stories cannot happen again. When we consume the broadcast messages of others we receive

---

[24] Only Cinema, in my opinion will continue to thrive. The introduction of digital cinemas will allow for greater audience immersion and the huge on-screen impact is not replicable on other screen devices. Going to the cinema remains a markedly different and deliberate kind of human activity.

Global Media Consumption per Week

Average hours per week.

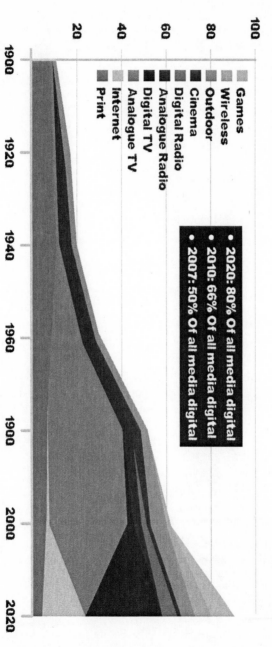

Games
Wireless
Outdoor
Cinema
Digital Radio
Analogue Radio
Digital TV
Analogue TV
Internet
Print

- 2020: 80% Of all media digital
- 2010: 66% Of all media digital
- 2007: 50% Of all media digital

100
80
60
40
20

1900
1920
1940
1960
1900
2000
2020

Source: Carat © World Association of Newspapers 2007-2008

them in small chunks, delivered fast. The messages we can't receive (due to the lack of time) are just blurred messages.

So we have an interesting duality of media consumption. On the one hand, the obsessive pursuit of intense detail and on the other a blurring of what else is out there. To make sense of this we have become our own editors, choosing what to allow onto our personalized TV schedules and smartphone "blink-feeds".

We trust ourselves and our own private perspectives on life to be good editors to our "audience of one" and we delight in the telling to others of things we have edited out and things we have edited in.

H.G. Wells would be surprised to discover that his World Encyclopedia was not so much the shared knowledge of all, for positive social use, but rather the noisy clamour of billions of messages about what we individually already know and do. Tweets to each other, shareable photographs, internalized discussion. It's now not a Net you reach out for. It's a Net you draw down from, in a process of relentless and literal cataloguing.

Robert Frank, the eminent American photographer, couldn't make sense of this when he added his own poetic voice to this "clamour" in a profile in *Vanity Fair*:[25] "There are too many images, too many cameras now. We're all being watched. It gets sillier and sillier. As if all action is meaningful. Nothing is really all that special. It's just life. If all moments are recorded, then nothing is beautiful and maybe photography isn't an art anymore. Maybe it never was."

---

[25] *Vanity Fair*, April 2008: Robert Frank's Unsentimental Journey, by Charlie LeDuff.

But his perspective was from an age when you travelled out and visited art galleries or bought art books. Today all art is within arm's reach, from your children's handmade birthday card, through Banksy to da Vinci. Each of these can be equally dignified by creating our own, individual "Book of My Own Art". If it's valid to me. It's valid. Period.

When we inevitably move 100% from "shared single global experience" to "shareable fragments of personal experience", the media outside becomes a mess for artists, programmers, marketers and purchasers. Where to be on TV? How to communicate? How to get more followers?

For content providers things are only going to get tougher. For us individuals, Channel Me is only going to get richer.

5 Streaming Screenagers.

Our sexuality, ethnicity, habitat, age and income are no longer our defining barriers. We are all "screenagers", happily addicted to an internalized screen-based pursuit.

Let's start with a simple observation.

How often do you see people walking down the street looking at the screens on their mobile phones? How often do you inadvertently bump into them as they stop short to scrutinize a message or image and at the same time you reach into your pocket to review the buzz of a received message?

If you have kids, do they "watch" TV, check messaging and stay glued to Facebook, for example, all at the same time?

Are you saying, "It's what the kids do", when you know you're increasingly doing it yourself?[26]

In meetings do you note the Ceremony of the Smart Phones as each is laid neatly next to the pad, where the pencil once sat? And when I say pad I mean iPad, of course.[27]

Have you noticed how the ping of someone else's phone will snap them back to their screen even mid-conversation and cause you to briefly check your own phone for any change in any messaging status?

Do you walk into spaces (train stations, airport lounges, subways, kitchens) and see people staring into their tablets and e-readers?

Are your kids upstairs right now feverishly fingering their games consoles, completely lost in a magical screen world?

We all know this is happening. Let's put some figures to these observations.[28]

ABI Research predicts that in 2013 the annual volume of smartphone app downloads will exceed 56 billion.[29] Phone and tablet apps have provided us with fast and fun shortcut navigation of our screens. They take us to where we want to be in an instant. No wonder we choose to travel through them as regularly as we can.

---

[26] http://www.entrepreneur.com/blog/225718#ixzz2UzYZC59b. More than 80% of 18- to 24-year-olds told Pew Research they used their phone while watching TV, and 60% of Americans above $50,000 use their phones while watching TV.

[27] http://www.businessinsider.com/ipads-dominate-tablet-usage-2013-5#ixzz2V50fFvTZ. The iPad family accounted for 81% of tablet use in the U.S. and Canada during April 2013.

[28] A study by Lookout Mobile Security.

[29] http://www.abiresearch.com/press/android-will-account-for-58-of-smartphone-app-down

Some 54% of us check our phones while in bed — before we go to sleep, after we wake up or in the middle of the night. And one in five checks immediately after sex!

Nearly 40% check their phones while on the toilet. Toilet texting ("turfing") is particularly popular among 28 to 35-years-old, with a reported 91% of that age group admitting to the habit, a study by 11mark reveals.

An unabashed 30% of us check our phones during a meal with others, and 9% check their phones during religious services.

An entire industry has grown up to service this new screen age, termed "second screen". Second screen technology aims to both add to and enhance screen viewing.

Nielson's "Global Online Consumers and Multi-Media Usage" report of May 2012 surveyed more than 28,000 Internet respondents in 56 countries throughout Asia-Pacific, Europe, Latin America, the Middle East, Africa and North America. The survey was limited in only one way, in that it provided a perspective on only the habits of existing Internet users, not total populations.

Usage and Growth in online and mobile technologies*

Watched video content at least once a month.

COMPUTER AT HOME	TV AT HOME	ONLINE (ANY DEVICE)	MOBILE PHONE	
86	90	70	55	2010
84	83	74	90	2011

Source: Nielson Global Survey of multi-screen media usage, Q3 2011
*As represented by Online Consumers

But it supplies the data that supports our observations. Look at the difference a year makes in the growth of online and mobile video consumption. While at first glance it looks as if it is at the expense of home viewed content, we have already seen in the previous chapter that it is not necessarily at the expense of TV channel-produced material.

Thanks to the growth of smart phones and tablets, entertainment consumption on mobile devices has grown 82% from 2010 to 2011.[30] This growth outstripped the 55% growth of smart phones over the same period.

Worldwide, screens are our interaction with more than entertainment. They are our outlook on other people, they are our information centres and they are a major perspective on the world. They connect us in a way we couldn't physically be connected before. They search for us in a new and exciting way. And they elevate our lives way above the claustrophobia of only being in one place at a time.

What we are observing is a significant and sustained change in behaviour. We have all become screenagers.

The seeing, sending and sharing of snippets of film, one-off photos, Tweets, instant messages and so on, is not just omnipresent, it is homogeneous. We are all behaving in the same way.

For many people the opportunity to communicate screen-to-screen offers a level of desired control. It is a control of personality. Edited messages allow for brevity of thought without the fear of further engagement. Committing yourself to free-form conversation can in

---

[30] Source: Millennial Media and comScore.

certain circumstances be much more hazardous than packaging and sending small thoughts or ideas.

For others it offers a doorway to reach out widely – more widely than you ever could in the real analogue world. This type of reaching out might be a valuable opening – a lifeline – for the lonely and isolated; but it might also be making people more isolated as research worldwide is beginning to suggest.[31]

Just as we laud the power of the screens to link us so easily with "friends", evidence is emerging that screenagers heavily dependent on social networks can feel lonelier and are becoming lazier.

In an implosive force the more matter is driven together the less the actual relationships between each individual piece of matter have individuality and relevance. In fact they coalesce. They merge and meld. We may think that we are exploding out our social circles but in fact we are more likely to be integrating true friends with less-true friends and sending them all homogenous small-sized parcels of ourselves in a claustrophobic miasma of public/personal relationships. More links to more people means more time looking into more lives through snaps, chats, likes and one-line comments.

We are being taken somewhere new. Somewhere we haven't been before and somewhere we didn't think we could ever get to. We are actually able to travel through the lives of others.

Whereas "pre-Web" it was physical social interaction that gave us our customer profiles and personal identification, now it is how we choose to behave through our screens

---

[31] A national survey by Relationship Australia, July 2011
http://www.mobiledia.com/news/99729.html
and Spanish Centre for Sociological Investigations (CIS), June 2012
http://www.searchgi.com/article/The-Internet-Makes-People-Isolated

that defines us.

In fact social interaction per se has declined as our use of electronic media has increased.

See this graph below, produced for the EU by Dr Aric Sigman.[32]

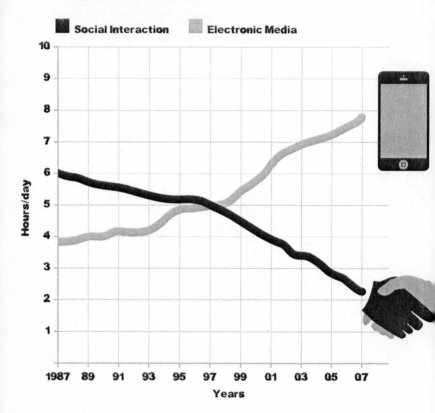

Hours per day of face-to-face social interaction declines as use of electronic media increase. The trends are predicted to increase (data abstracted from a series of time-use and demographic studies). (Sigman, 2009)

---

[32] *The Impact Of Screen Media On Children: A Eurovision For Parliament* by Dr. Aric Sigman, Health Education Lecturer, Fellow of the Society of Biology, Associate Fellow of the British Psychological Society.

Ten years ago where we lived, what we wore, our age, income and sexuality all sent out clear signals to marketers and broadcasters. Today, we are increasingly being defined by invisible and weightless notions. Where you live does not matter when your screen needs no address. What we are wearing can now no longer accurately pin us down when we can communicate invisibly. Even our age and sexuality can be concealed, or amended, as we sculpt each interaction according to what is required.

Today we are becoming shaped by what we choose to consume from the Internet, not by the previous, and often imposed, theories of social structures.

All screenagers start their Internet life on an equal footing with everyone else.

Regina Guthold of the World Health Organization noted that by the time a child is seven years old, they have already spent one whole year staring at screens.[33] Not surprisingly most observers of this fact foresee an even greater intensity in our relationship with the world through the screen.[34]

The dominant screens are now smart phones and tablets. Obviously these devices take the consumption of content out of the home. Now you can watch anything anywhere.

Like snacking on the go, we consume bite-sized Internet content on the go.

We can cleverly create content on the go as well, seeing something we like then sending Instagram or Snap Chat snapshots across the world instantly. We'll check and

---

[33] Physical Activity and Sedentary Behavior Among Schoolchildren: A 34-Country Comparison, *Journal of Pediatrics*, July 2010.

[34] There is much conjecture that the increase in "screen consumption" is directly linked to the rapid increase in child obesity. If true, it becomes another evidential part of the story of the inwardness of the direction of the Internet.

double check immediately to see if anyone "liked" the photo.

In 2011, Mark Zuckerberg, the founder of Facebook, described the new developments which would allow for "real-time serendipity in a friction-less experience". Frictionless sharing is making it effortless to share anything. Anything at all.

The only editor is yourself. And let's be honest, we're not all going to be great content editors when the audience is someone other than yourself. But when the audience is *only* yourself, you see your self-edited screen in the only justifiable light you can see it in – your own.

How many times have you been asked to share a post, Tweet, photo or whatever only to receive back something that you didn't really need, or want to receive?

Worse. How often have you posted something which you later regret for its obvious lack of interest or its blatant and spirited indiscretion!

Instagram posts offer a useful guide to the type of content we consume. Mashable.com has kindly listed them for us:

Feet on the beach,

Interesting cloud formations,

Food we are about to eat,

Finger and toenail art,

Inspirational quotations,

Tall buildings shot from the ground,

Designs on café lattes,

Our sms conversations,

Aircraft window views of airplane wing,

Bathroom mirror selfies,

Circle of feet,

Sunsets. [35]

Come on own up. How many of these have you been possessed to take in a moment of pure self-absorption? We all do it. And there's an obvious logic as to why.

They are all snapshots of our intimate relationship to the outside world. Our bodies, the sky and what we eat. Rarely do we see these snaps break out in a pioneering observation of "the unknown" or "the new".

Cyberspace is now full of such debris. It is full of what individuals like, not necessarily what is liked by consensus, or expert opinion. It is debris, because we create it and discard it very quickly and leave it lying about.

In fact we now continuously peer into our screens to audit response data from our connected others. The lack of response can make a huge impact and conspire to create a huge burden.

Those more proficient in managing the various applications that now sort and sift screen responses will

---

[35] http://mashable.com/2012/08/31/cliche-instagram-photos/

often deliberately and very strategically up-weight their Web of connections just to ensure their broadcasts are "liked" or to be confident of a response from someone. Somewhere. And in the worst-case scenario?

Anyone.

The screens are now an important portal into the world. They connect us with family, friends and colleagues who are not immediately present in our lives and it could be argued that one of the more impressive contributions the Internet has made to our lives is that now we can all be contemporaneously connected.

In our analogue past we connected with people in a more formal and organized way. We shared real photographs and exchanged thoughts verbally. The writing of a letter was a considered act. It was also quite expensive and awkward. You had to buy paper, a pen and a stamp. It took time.

Now talk is cheap. For most people data packages are constructed in a way that the cost of a Facebook message or Snap Chat is considered to be free.

Screenagers now operate freely in two senses of the word. They are free to travel wherever they wish and they are free to communicate at what is considered to be no cost at all.

Contemporaneous Connectivity has tethered us all to the communities and individuals we want to be joined to. Being addicted to our screens has created an explosion of connectivity and at the same time a fear of lack of connection. Again we see the Internet initially carrying us out on an explosive journey only to find that in reality it has tied us together in the tightest of all nets. These are nets of our existing worlds, our universes of friends and interests and they must be scrutinized and monitored at all times.

The Internet hasn't just allowed you to travel. It's allowed everyone else to travel to you. Whenever they wish. Uninvited, if they so choose.

The contemporaneous connectivity of our screen lives is fed by what I call "universal content". Universal content is made up of essentially four component parts: instant information, snippets of film, byte-sized messages and one-off snapshots of people, food or views, or feet…

Personal consumption (ie, the consumption of screen content that you don't feel you need to share) is increasingly the domain of tablets and comprises the reading of books and the watching of movies.

We are consuming the same individually created diet, day in day out.

I make and emphasize this point because it's important. The invention of television has genuinely widened people's available repertoire of viewing content. But we all watched essentially the same thing.

The invention of the Internet has genuinely enhanced people's access to the repertoire of our daily existence. And we are all watching different things on different screens.

Our screens today, with access to a massive amount of content, are confining us into essentially the same circle of self-edited data. And so it will remain, because we now have permission and access to plunder all that ever was, is and will be out there.

Screenagers are of all ages, are to be found amongst all socio-demographic backgrounds, cut through continents and cultures and are not bound by similarities of religion.

They are not a target demographic by usual standards but advertisers obviously want to reach them. They do this by watching and responding to their individual online behaviour.

Every time we peer into our screens, transmit and receive information, that self-same information is being gathered, analyzed and converted to algorithms.

When, for example, you sign Facebook's terms and conditions (a longer document to plough through than the United States Constitution) you agree to this.

So advertisers watch and analyze what we are digesting online and feed it straight back to us through online advertising. They can look at demographics, passions and interests (based on download behaviour) and context (location, time of the day you did something, type of screen device you are using, etc, etc). It's fast and targeted to how we behave.

This turns upside down the conventional theory of targeting.

Once upon a time, you selected your target audience (say, women, aged 25-50, with kids, living in rural locations) then found the right medium to connect with them.

But does Amazon target in this way? Does Amazon care about exactly who buys what from them?

No. Amazon has created an online process that makes purchasing a large number of items effortless.

It's the process that has come first, not the customer segmentation.

Amazon welcomes anybody in through their screen and only then does it start watching what you buy. Amazon's front door to your shop is YOUR screen. Watching you allows Amazon to market things to your preference profile and helps them facilitate for you a wider portfolio of products.

Screens take you to many retail front doors, big and small, without requiring you to know how long they have been in business, how large a store they are or, indeed, if anyone else shops there. If it's brought to you, and you like it, that's all you need to think about. This gives a huge competitive advantage to new retail start-ups. But again, the winners win not because they have targeted a particular demographic segment, but because they have targeted an existing need and delivered it in a weightless, effortless, fluid way.

Once we didn't go to shops that didn't have what we wanted. Now, we don't go to sites that don't deliver fluidity of process. We KNOW they can deliver what we want.

Plotting how all screenagers behave will ultimately be the plotting of how we all behave. The data gives an introspective view on the immediate past and punts an offering based on a copycat purchasing future.

Imprinting deeds already done onto a future imagined (and hoped), creates an implosive identikit of the past.

In fact, in an act of breathtaking implosive bravado, coders work hard to ensure that we don't break out randomly into new places. They need us to do more of the same so they can deliver advertisers neatly to our screen doors. In turn we oblige by feeding our behavioural patterns back into the algorithm, buying, behaving and being a more complete, self-defined version of the person we were before we opened up our screens.

What does it mean to see us all "heads in screens" as we go about our business and our daily lives?

It means we are being increasingly more defined versions of "ourselves". Goodbye "demographic profiling". Hello "you make MY life easier to navigate".

And "thank you, you have bothered to think about me and contributed to a smoother flowing of MY life".

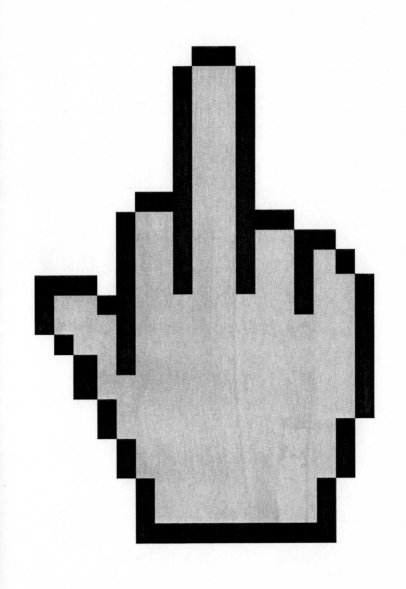

6 Socialism, Socializing and Being Social.

The World Wide Web is a new form of global democracy, but not the kind that many had hoped. It is increasingly a highly monitored, analyzed space where every single person's view has to be taken at face value. Problem is, you can't always see the face.

There can be no doubt that the World Wide Web provides a forum for freedom of speech, thought and action.

Besides the tsunami of self-published dictums on Twitter, Facebook, LinkedIn, Huffington Post et al, there is a minute-by-minute torrent of messaging and comment. The Tweeting of other people's personal information held under "super-injunctions"; the Tweeting of personal views on people you have never met; the release of "sensitive" government information through Wikileaks and the cross border complexities of what is legal to publish and what isn't, all demonstrate that the Web is a powerful, carefree and unrestrained communication vehicle.

As Eric Schmidt, Google's Executive Chairman, puts it: "(The Internet) is the world's largest ungoverned space."

Marx and Engels might well muse that today the power is in the screens of the people. The thing is, we are all screenagers. "The People" is no longer a political sub-set. It is all of us.

Everyone has migrated, together, to a new space with all the social statuses, identity baggage and economic opportunities they had grown to develop or had previously held in a pre-Internet life.

But this new space is not, as its effortless ubiquitous availability suggests, a technological democracy, despite its apparent open access.

Sure, it can collect and collate people who choose to be drawn together by shared ideals. And some indeed are drawn by notions of "a priori" core democratic principles – such as the right to life; personal, political, economic and religious freedom; justice; equality; and government of the people.

But in truth, not many.

Depending on your definition of "democratic", the Internet holds a rainbow collection of assertive sites, like Avaaz, "a campaigning community bringing people-powered politics to decision-making worldwide".[36] Avaaz has over 17 million members of its "movement". There are countless others, many national based such as the UK's 38 degrees with a more modest 1 million members and the USA's partisan pro-Democrat MoveOn.org with over 3 million.

But these are small numbers when you consider there are some 2.5 billion people accessing the Internet. Only 27% of the Internet is conducted in English, with almost the same again in Chinese.[37] The Internet is, in fact, becoming multi-ethnic and increasingly Asian,[38] but whoever and wherever we are, we still choose to gather around the same virtual water holes.

These billions coalesce around:

Facebook	*Wikipedia*
Google	*Windows Live*
YouTube	*Twitter*
Yahoo!	*QQ*
Baidu	*Amazon*

...ie, Internet usage is predominantly based on straightforward ordinary behaviour – chitchat, shopping and entertainment. The high ranking of Wikipedia might suggest that H.G. Wells' hopes of a World Encyclopaedia were coming to fruition, but a closer analysis reveals that

---

[36] http://www.avaaz.org/en/

[37] Internet World Stats.

[38] ibid. Over 31% of the top ten languages are represented by Asian languages.

Wikipedia is used in a much more introspective way. In 2012, the most viewed subject in English on Wikipedia was Facebook, with, wait for it, the second most viewed Wikipedia article being…Wikipedia.[39]

Just think for a minute. The Internet gives us huge privileges of knowledge gathering, but we are herded into a small number of vast stockades.

By whom?

By ourselves. We choose to travel to the places where our friends are.

We are driven to the same places as everyone else, often matching their behaviour, certainly learning from each other, becoming experts of each other's Internet lives.

It would not feel at all like liberty if we felt we were told to go there and nowhere else, but no one is telling us to do anything. A few owners running vast estates corralling us back in when we leave, through the many hooks (cookies, etc) that we have unwittingly agreed to attach ourselves to might sound like the aristocracies of the past, but that is not what is happening.

Conventional words for societal structure (democracy, theocracy, plutocracy, socialism, republicanism, oligarchy and so on) seem weak against the effortless influence of the Internet to transform and enhance day-to-day personal activities.

We have created our own worlds and in so doing are creating an "atomocracy", a government of one. A movement of one. An indivisible, individualistic culture, with its own views on matters of law, liberties, state and religion.

---

[39] http://toolserver.org/~johang/2012.html

No, the Net is not a democratic state. That can only be achieved by human will, not by the powerful processors, protocol and software that make up the World Wide Web.

Wishing that the Web might spread democracy is just that – wishful thinking. As a dream it has created a confusion of hope over what (particularly) social media can do when harnessed to open-access information. Essentially campaigning social media sites combine advocacy with mobilization of forces and some kind of required action, usually online petitioning.

So has the Web harnessed a new collective and collaborative "people power"?

It is fair to say that the global nature of, for example, Avaaz's membership is a new phenomenon. In pre-Internet days it was much harder to create global movements quickly and even harder to communicate to every member.

There have been notable exceptions of course.

The physical demolition of the Berlin Wall on 9th November 1989 was fuelled by a mass movement of shared belief and consciousness and it spread quickly. It was further fuelled by CNN and the BBC World Service, the latter affording a more clandestine news update through secreted radios. With "Glasnost", the BBC, Deutsche Welle and Voice of America were heard legitimately in the USSR and like a rolling snowball the movement gathered in momentum and size, eroding pro-Soviet political power in its path. This pre-Internet phenomenon was remarkable for the physicality of the demolition. Here were ordinary people, wielding pick-axes, actually knocking out bricks and concrete from the

Wall. Those were the images to record and remember. Those images ignited an explosion of genuine, tangible, change, the ripples of which are still being felt today.

In 2012 there was another large-scale movement. It was global and it came to the attention of almost 100 million people.

Kony2012 was a mass movement of people (young people in the main), who were struck by an online film made by Invisible Children. The film wanted Joseph Kony, an indicted war criminal and fugitive, to be bought to justice.

Very quickly Kony2012 became an Internet sensation with over 93 million views on YouTube. There was real excitement about the actions people were taking. Kony became known in schools, universities, offices and homes across the globe. Everyone was talking about it. The campaign was to build to a climax called "Cover the Night". This was, like the demolition of the Wall, an opportunity for everybody to be engaged, globally, in a physical way by papering the walls of their towns with images of the Ugandan warlord.

The potential for powerful imagery, of the order of the pick-axes on top of the Berlin Wall, was huge. Imagine waking up the next morning to see hundreds of thousands of images of Kony pinned up around cities all over the world. All it required was for people to transfer their virtual on-screen support to physical on-street support.

But the campaign imploded. There were paltry turnouts in the USA, Australia and Europe, where the heat of the online campaign was centered. Sadly, the movement's credibility was seriously damaged.

Twitter provided a reason why: "What happened to all the fuss about Kony?" said one typical Tweet. "Kony is so last month," said another.

No explosion of long lasting change and deep-rooted effect. Just a spiralling down of enthusiasm as everyone's attention was drawn to the Next Big Thing.

The demolition of the Berlin Wall was preceded and encouraged by Mikhail Gorbacev's *Perestroika* and *Glasnost*. It is not the remit of this book to go into that much-recorded moment in history except to observe that from the grassroots unrest in Poland in the early '80s there was a movement of many people supplying wind to the sails that Gorbachev was putting up. It took time – almost ten years – but a significant re-ordering of democratic principles across a huge swathe of the globe came into being.

Many observers today look to the Internet as the central, key agent to bring about similar democratic change in other parts of the world. In fact the "Arab Spring" has been cited to have happened *because* of the Internet.

Certainly the immediate transmission of video and comment from the front lines of Tunisia and Egypt were compelling. Oppressive regimes were toppled by protesters organized via Twitter and Facebook and utilizing new technology offered through smart phones.

As Peter Godspeed noted: "New technology apparently shifted the balance of power in favour of the world's repressed."[40] In theory we can expect an explosion of

---

[40] http://fullcomment.nationalpost.com/2012/04/21/goodspeed-analysis-governments-could-soon-record-and-store-everything-their-citizens-do-from-birth-to-death/

Internet-fuelled uprisings.

Marx and Engels are now sitting up and taking notice.

But the opposite is happening. Whereas, once upon a long time ago, experienced journalists reported and posted (often literally putting paper into a post box) eyewitness accounts of unfolding events, now every device with a screen sends, and, importantly, is sent, un-edited footage and comment. These images often appear, similarly un-edited, on mainstream broadcast news channels.

But it's hard to distinguish one source from another, because in an atomocracy the source has the power to deceive, obfuscate and confuse.

So the Internet supplies reality and fake in equal measure and in so doing devalues the currency and potency of "reported news".

The Internet is everybody's tool. One man's Twitter feed is equal to another's. One child's Facebook post is another despot's Instagram pic.

In fact, because of the prevalence of Internet-related messaging, authorities are now embracing the new media possibilities and, as Goodspeed goes on to remark, "the Arab Spring may have ushered in a new culture of control in which governments — from democracies to dictatorships — may soon be able to exploit new technologies to monitor entire populations in order to target and destroy all dissent".[41]

Again, what initially appears to be a dynamic opportunity for openness and change almost immediately becomes an

---

[41] ibid.

equal opportunity for tyranny, introspection and control.

For example, during Iran's 2009 Green Revolution, the Revolutionary Guard effectively monitored cellphone traffic and activity on social media Internet sites such as Twitter and Facebook to identify and arrest anti-government ringleaders.[42]

The Internet/smart phone uprisings lack the long determined progress of Glasnost and Perestroika. They flare up, implode, flare, implode with a remarkable haste and eventually, like Kony, lose their energy.

"What's next after Tunisia" I imagine a tweet saying.

"Who cares?"

If there is a democratization happening it is the democratization of all the bytes sent to our devices. It is perfectly valid to switch from horror to fun with a swipe of the finger.

"Charlie-bit-my-fingerism" now enjoys equal status with, and probably draws a higher level of attention than, socialism as a Web page to enjoy. And why not? An atomocracy has its own unique billions of social mores and culture-defining snapshots of what's in and what's out.

Our large Internet communities enjoy new things and have the power to let them spiral down to inconsequence once the new "new" arrives.

To find the biggest communities on the Web you have to look at sites that are agnostic about change, be it social, environmental, political or ethical.

---

[42] ibid.

The biggest player on the Internet today is Facebook.

If Facebook were a country, its one billion-plus citizens (or "netizens") would make it the third largest country in the world. Yet the personal information this "new-era State" holds on each citizen is of unparalleled detail. The depth and breadth of the information (a small part of which includes birth dates, addresses, photos of you, photos of your friends, how your family is constructed, what you are thinking, when and where you go to when you leave your house) is a level of surveillance that even the most optimistic members of the Cold War's East German Ministry for State Security (the Stasi) could never have dreamed of.

This level of surveillance goes beyond real-time recording of what people are saying and extends to the tracking and analysis of all past activity.

The netizens of Facebook, in the main, accept this level of observation and surveillance as the price they pay for free, fluid, effortless, global interconnectivity.

Today we happily give away freedoms in return for open access into and out of our lives. The hunters, fishers and farmers of 5,000BC would stand back aghast.

It's not just Facebook that is able to profile our actions. All the traces we leave behind on the Internet are just as identifiable.

We "move through" the Internet with a freedom of passage that is completely logged. It is a cyberspace estate that offers freedom with one hand but takes anonymity with another. And what drives it is our open desire to willingly participate and share.

This willingness is what drives the content and what, to a large extent, drives out the earnest desires for the Web to be a "global democratic power-base".

On the Web, conventional political forces (socialism, fascism, conservatism, liberalism, republicanism, for example) have ceded their intellectual importance to Charlie-bit-my-fingerism and a new, generalized, self-generated and widely accepted global web dialogue has now emerged.

Political groups, governments and oppositions have all flocked to the Web. There's no surprise there. But their messages are met with more counter views than ever before. That's good you may say. Democracy is alive and well. But that's not democracy. That's noise. Real noise. Fake noise. Controlled noise. Uncontrolled noise. Modern democracy is government by the eligible people of a country, exercised through elected representatives.

In an atomocracy there are no elections. Your vote carries your message and so does everyone else's. Your comment attracts other comment. Other individuals are drawn in. There is a concentration of comment. Then it swiftly moves on to the next attractive, likeable comment. Think of it as explosion of comment followed by implosion of attraction.

It is in this context that, in my view, the debate about the discovery of "Prism" in early June 2013 has been misplaced. Prism is the previously unknown program run in the United States by the National Security Agency (NSA) to access data held by the world's major Internet companies, including Facebook, Google, Microsoft, Apple, Yahoo and Skype.

We all give up our data in return for freedom of online passage. Equally we understand we have the power to speak and judge freely as we see fit on people, places and products. There will inevitably be a generational skew. Teens, for example, are sharing more information about themselves on social media sites than they have in the past, but they are also taking a variety of technical and non-technical steps to manage the privacy of that information. Despite taking these privacy-protective actions, teen social media users do not express a high level of concern about third-parties (such as businesses or advertisers) accessing their data.[43]

The furore about the discovery of Prism has been handled in a pre-Internet analogue way. Prism has been castigated as a Big Brother tool watching us all in intense detail.

But Big Brother belongs to our analogue past. It belongs in the world of Broadcasting, "Us and Them" and mass-communication.

That was a world of self-imposed "keep-yourself-to-yourself" privacy and almost no personal passwords and login details. Internet surveillance is actually the trawling through data we have all freely given. It is the piece-by-piece analysis of millions of atomocracies.

It is no wonder that, just a few days after the revelation that Prism existed, a majority of the sample of the United States public polled by The Pew Research Center and The Washington Post said that they were happy for the authorities to investigate terrorism, even if it intruded on personal privacy. [44]

---

[43] Just 9% say they are "very" concerned, according to Pew Internet Research, 21st May 2013.

[44] Pew Research Center for the People and the Press, 10th June 2013.

Giving our personal data is now no longer a "shall we, shan't we" issue. As we consume the net we do it naturally. As naturally as our digestive systems step in when we start to consume food.

The discussion about Prism is taking place as one world order (analogue) cedes to another (digital). Factions from both sides are playing their roles accordingly.

But there can be only one outcome.

As our individual atomocracies take hold and strengthen, we will progressively care less about how our data is used.

On the contrary, in a reversal of the analogue model, we will supply more data if it liberates us to edit in and out the things that we feel will improve our lives. Prism is now the poster-child of data manipulation and the beginning of a long road to re-define the term "personal-freedoms".

Over the years I have encountered much confusion between the socializing effect of the Internet (mainly, but not exclusively through social networks) and the belief in a new form of Net socialism. There is very little evidence to suggest that the parcelling-up of millions of global citizens into specific places is causing them to think more positively about each other.

Whilst good thinkers and doers might link and act together around specific aims, so do the Internet trolls who post inflammatory and usually off-message content, causing considerable distress. Freedom has its price, we have now surely learned? But we continue to consider it a price worth paying.

Socializing through the Net compounds and compacts offline socializing and drives a desire for a regular diet of new tit-bits at an accelerating rate. It is taste driven. That is, individual tastes. These tastes can now be ordered and compounded and shared, sculpting well defined individual features regardless of whether others find them attractive or not, as was witnessed by the "oil and water" differences of opinion over Baroness Thatcher's time as UK Prime Minister.

Socialism might be defined as a system whereby the means of production and distribution is in the hands of the community for direct use of products and services rather than profit.

Social networks do almost the complete opposite, proliferating the mass production and distribution of individual agendas. Groupon, for example, harnesses individuals to produce greater personal profit through maximization of discounts.

If anything, in another implosive detonation, social networks will begin to give way to Personal Networks, sparking another power-shift altogether.

7 Being Present.

The Internet has made selling goods simpler. So why isn't doing business simpler for companies? Because anyone, anywhere can now sell. It's a level playing field for big and small alike and you have to fight harder than ever to be noticed.

A visit to John Wanamaker's new department store in Philadelphia in 1871 would have been like no other visit to any other kind of store anywhere else in the world. He had real stand out. His store was a destination like none other. Everybody was gossiping about it, reading about it and getting excited about it. Mr. Wanamaker had a serious Unique Selling Proposition.

As it happens, John Wanamaker was already a department store pioneer, had been for many years – heck, he'd even invented the price tag (it was shopping-by-haggling before that); but this was way different. Today we'd call it a "paradigm shift" or a "game changer".

If there was no room inside, crowds would stand outside the store just to have the opportunity to see what the buzz was all about and be a part of it. Families came as well; little ones perched high on their parent's shoulders.

This was a massive moment.

Wanamaker was "Being Present".

Wanamaker's competitors were nowhere. All they could do was stand and watch too, as customers flooded into his store.

Today, the progressive UK retailer John Lewis now has the self same wonder product that John Wanamaker had. In fact they both share many common attributes. They both have a legacy of trust and the promises they make are true. But John Lewis gains no competitive advantage from Wanamaker's innovation because that wonder product today, still brilliant in conception, still dazzling in delivery, still enlightened in so many ways, is now so commonplace it might as well be invisible.

Today every store has the electric light.

In fact all of us are all connected by the medium of

electricity, creating an equal opportunities market place.

Once they saw the effect it had on business, it didn't take long for Wanamaker's competitors to install electricity.

120 years later and a few brave pioneers took to the Internet like a fish to water. One of the first known Web purchases took place in 1994, when Pizza Hut sold its first online pizza – a pepperoni pizza with mushrooms and extra cheese. Of course, we know every detail of that purchase and all subsequent ones since!

With some ups and downs over approximately 15 years, eventually all businesses have been able to reach out to the Internet, grab it by the throat and install it into the very hearts of their organizations. As I watched an industry of "Web agencies" self-ignite, grow, develop and eventually spawn multi-variants and specialisms, it felt like I was watching the arrival of a new body part that would make humans faster and smarter. This body part needed specialists to perform the delicate operation of inserting it into living, breathing organisms. Once inserted, we would be different and we would acquire a new bodily function. The specialists were learning to perform the operation as they went along. This procedure was so new, hardly anyone had been taught how to do it.

We have witnessed an extraordinary phenomenon. A completely new industry – with no reference to the past – has sprung up and established itself in every country of this planet and the growth in number, and the growing professionalism, of the experts at work is impressive.

An industry of self-taught young people flashed instantaneously into existence and companies queued at their doors like eager patients waiting to be next for the treatment. Many would pay big money to queue-jump or get the best specialist there was available.

Businesses just took it. Many, I remember, weren't sure what they were taking it for. They just had to have it.

Of course, just about anyone who has access to electricity has access to the Internet. You can fairly equate the early pioneer Jeff Bezos of Amazon.com to Wanamaker; his first mover advantage has created the perfect online retailer.

Amazon has been learning about the changing demands of online retail since the day they first opened on 16th July 1995. Poignantly the first book sold on Amazon was Douglas Hofstadter's *Fluid Concepts and Creative Analogies: Computer Models of the Fundamental Mechanisms of Thought*. It has been fluid concepts and creative analogies that have kept Amazon as market leader. It constantly refines and develops itself, as it understands that the entrance to its store will soon be on every screen on the planet.

Forbes estimates that online sales today are growing at approximately ten times the rate of brick and mortar stores,[45] although in 2013 they still remain at a significantly lower percentage of all retail sales.[46]

There are a large number of books, websites and consultants doing a good job of explaining to businesses how to do e-commerce, how to maximize presence on social media, how to optimize search and so on.

I'm not going to add to them.

My observations about this are framed within the context

---

[45] http://www.forbes.com/sites/lisaarthur/2013/03/12/which-is-better-for-retail-sales-online-or-offline-customer-engagement/

[46] http://www.smartinsights.com/. Overall percentage of Ecommerce retail sales are perhaps, surprisingly small at around 5% of sales in the US and 10% in the UK, but with sustained growth. The data for Europe suggests growth rates of 10 to 20%.

of Homo Sapiens' new bodily function (consuming the Internet).

I'm suggesting that we consume the Internet as narcissistic "screenagers" in an "atomocracy".

We are consuming different things, personalized to our own tastes and free from the disapproving (and sometimes approving!) looks of others.

Our screens let us in freely to almost anywhere we fancy going.

So where are we going?

Aggregating the habits of individual's Internet usage over a month paints a general, but informative, picture. [47]

22% of our time is spent social networking
(eg, Facebook),

21% our time is spent on "search" mode
(eg, Google),

20% our time is spent absorbing content
(eg, YouTube),

19% our time is spent in communication
(eg, email, messaging),

13% our time is spent on multi media sites
(eg, Spotify)

and finally…

5% of our time is spent online shopping
(eg, Amazon).

---

[47] http://www.go-gulf.com/blog/online-time/

The first mover advantage of Amazon, iTunes and eBay has kept them at the top of online retailing.

It is no surprise then that in order to "be present" in customers' online minds, businesses must utilize as much of the remaining 95% of online space as possible to advertise their message and score what advantage they can from the dominant players.

But advertising where you think people will be was fine in an analogue, pre-Internet existence, because people tended to be where you expected them to be. For example, at 11.00pm on a Monday, they were highly unlikely to be shopping and more likely to be switching the TV off and jumping into bed.

Today, at 11.00pm, you are highly likely to be jumping into bed, switching on your screen and shopping and chatting.

The forward motion of activity in pre-Internet days is now a reverse motion.

So simply replacing analogue communication patterns with a digital counterpart and hoping people will "see and/or hear" you are not enough in my view. As Nielsen Media Research (NMR) has pointed out, there are three key things an advertiser wants to know:[48] "How many ads did we run?" "Who exactly saw them?" "Did it work?"

And with current evaluation methods, it's surprisingly difficult to tell.

The Internet offers advertisers great scope for engaging with its customers beyond its online advertisements.

---

[48] http://www.nielsen.com/us/en/newswire/2009/does-online-advertising-deliver-the-target-audience.html

There is the possibility of quality story-telling via long-form films on YouTube, for example. Often called "virals", these do exactly what viruses do and infiltrate the cellular activity of Internet consumption. Some "virals" pass through the system unnoticed; others have the effect of making an individual sit up and take notice. Others might be so infectious they are passed on immediately and instantly infect an individual's close, online community.

"Virals" are an attempt to replicate the sumptuous and highly engaging TV and cinema advertising of (mainly) 1960-2000. These were well crafted and talked about.

But those were different times. I repeat, you cannot simply place analogue advertising memes into a digital space and expect to get the same result. Everything will be different. Including measurement.

Amazon doesn't communicate a well-crafted storyline on the Internet. It simply recognizes that its front door is the screen you happen to be holding. And it makes sure that your expectations of what is on offer are properly managed.

In a pre-Internet world, businesses needed to consider the "Five Ps", when marketing their product or service. Product, Price, Promotion, Place and People each responsibly represented an audit of marketing "must-haves". There are many variations on this, but essentially it all comes down to these five categories.

Did a company have the right product at the right price? Was it being promoted properly? Would customers find it in the right places and was it targeted to the needs of the right people?

It's a post-Internet world, so I'll add one more important P. "Presence".

Marketers need to understand the narcissistic way we consume our online diets.

We embrace and embroil an online shopping expedition into broader and deeper offline behaviour. And vice versa. We message friends for shopping and lunch/drinks advice. We pre-plan our offline journeys. Online we react spontaneously to on- and offline conversations and received wisdom. It's pure digital behaviour, not in the sense that it's Web-based, but in the sense that it's "bit-based". Our many small acts of individual processing amount to a significant journey towards where and how we spend our money.

This is where marketers need to look first. And this is where marketers need to review their use of the five (now six) "Ps".

In pre-Internet days a company told you its product has a USP so that it would attract you and make you want it. Today we see and hear that message at the same time as it is debated by competitors, comparison sites and communities, so its merits are clouded and creating uncertainty and lack of distinction.

Products and services today are more similar than ever before. They can be emulated at speed by competitors. Now companies simply have to make products that people want, rather than make people want products; and they have to get that product to the purchaser in a fluid, easy way.

In a reverse of the way things were, products need to

have individual desirability built in, not bolted on. It is not enough to mass-produce a product and just hope that thousands of people will enjoy owning the same things. Increasingly they do not – they are enjoying individual experiences. To do this, companies need to bring the expectations of the prospective purchaser into the capital cost stage and ask themselves this question:

Am I confident this product now inherently performs in a more interesting and desirable way than any other product out there?

If it doesn't, then capital expenditure on tooling and marketing, for example, will be wasted and no amount of clever communication will save it.

To build-in desirability companies need to change the way they view their customers. One thing you can learn from the Internet is how customers are behaving – the data is there in trends and actual visits. And it tells you about customer behaviour off- and online.

It wasn't so long ago that we professionally segmented and specified our targets. Now it's time to turn the marketing model upside down and note that it is customer behaviour, not customer segmentation that is providing the clues.

We are all in the same boat. Companies and customers alike are consuming the Internet together. In the customer's mind their screens, apps and favourite sites are their doorways into companies. Companies have no doorways any more. There is only one.

Bound together, in a totally new way, the relationship between company and customer is best served when it is on an equal footing. I don't expect to know the people finding and delivering my purchase from Amazon. And I wouldn't expect Amazon to spend millions of dollars advertising what they do. Why? Because I am at the Amazon door ready to buy what I have already chosen.

Service is now about delivery of expectations.

If I assume a company to have poor delivery, there is every expectation I will avoid it at all costs. Even if it is selling something I really want.

If I experience a company that has perfectly delivered a product that I bought effortlessly and which has a specific value to me personally, I will revisit that company and be prepared to enjoy almost anything it has to offer me. Hence Amazon's growth of product lines way beyond books, where it first started.

The value chain in the product starts with Inherent Difference, goes through Value and ends with Process.

Everyone has the Internet, just as everyone now has electricity. The Internet cannot itself create difference and it is a big mistake to think that just because a new product is launched as an "app", or cool-sounding website, for example, it will have immediate interest and visibility.

You gain presence through observing purchasing patterns and behaviour, building in genuine difference and making the purchasing process fluid and, in an ideal world, fun.

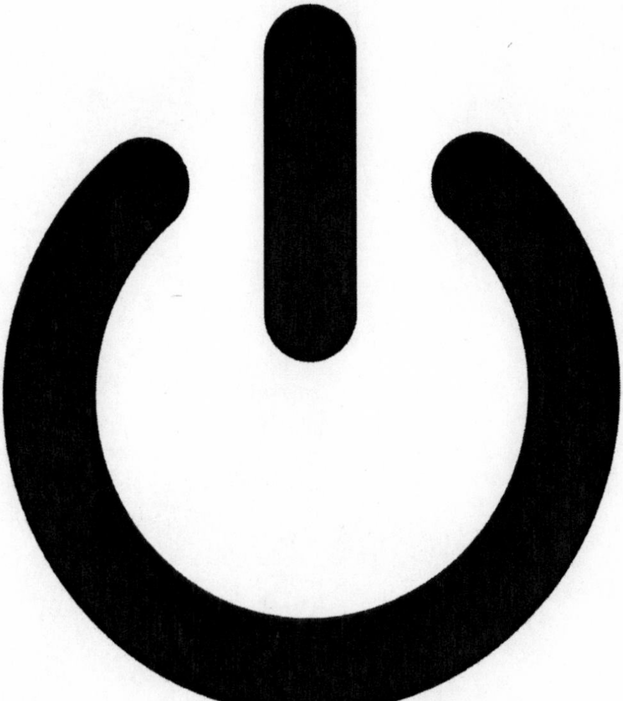

8 New Order.

The implosive effect of the Internet offers wonderful new opportunities for those that recognize the new dynamics and are prepared to change the way they work.

In the last chapter I talked about some basic marketing principles.

Now, marketing itself needs to be contextualized within an implosive environment.

The science of Marketing began at the beginning of the

last century. A certain Dr. E.D. Jones is often credited with creating the first course in Marketing in 1902 at the University of Michigan. This course was not actually called "Marketing" when it was first offered, but "The Distributive and Regulative Industries of the US". It was Ralph Starr Butler at the University of Wisconsin who actually delivered the first course, simply called "Marketing", some seven years later. Ralph's pioneering program was later compiled into a textbook, *Butler's Marketing Methods*, the tenets of which still remain the basis of modern advertising.

In the intervening period, other universities had nevertheless started providing their own courses on distribution, advertising, salesmanship and related subjects. [49]

A Google NGram of the word "marketing" demonstrates its growing 20th-century importance.

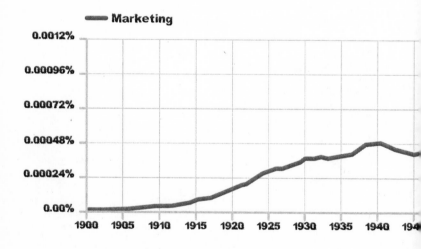

---

[49] *The History of Marketing Thought* by R. Bartels.

It was the 1960's that re-invigorated the science, with valuable contributions from Theodore Levitt, Lance Packard, Marshall McLuhan and the like.

Today there are over 116,000 books available to buy from Amazon on the subject of marketing and many thousands of high-quality courses to be taken the world over.

In 2005 I was asked to construct and teach a marketing course for Haier, China's largest white goods manufacturer (and thereby the largest white goods manufacturer in the world with an almost 8% share of the global market). Haier wanted to start at the beginning. They wanted first to learn the basics of marketing and then work out how these might be applied to their business. 2005 was the dawn of social networking and the Internet was still evolving. Like many companies around the world, Haier were not a highly evolved online company at that time

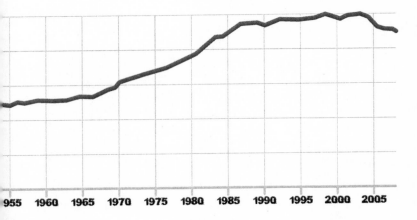

Google NGram

and so they felt it appropriate to start at the beginning.

The course I created was handed straight down from Jones, Levitt, McLuhan and the gang. Because the truth is that most of the original precepts of marketing still stand today.

Marketing is a commercial process. It involves positioning and promoting a product or service, as we saw in the previous chapter. Sometimes it involves distributing and selling too.

But you know all this.

You are almost certainly wondering where this is going.

It's going into the Digital Age.

The science of marketing has reached an interesting stage in its development. From smart selling tactics, through intelligent psychology to data driven analysis, marketing has evolved with a number of carefully considered stratagems.

And alongside its evolution, customers have evolved too. Twenty-five years ago it was clear that a significant percentage of the population could see through the marketers' stratagems. They could decipher the tactics being used and were learning how not to be unnecessarily confused or hoodwinked.

Then the Internet arrived.

In this last chapter I am going to consider the impact that the implosive force has had on the way businesses conduct commercial transactions.

And we start by looking at whom marketing departments target and how they do it.

Marketing departments don't see people as people. They see them as "consumers".

Consumers!

Apart from referencing the titles of research documents, this is the first time I have used the word "consumer" in this book.

That's because it aptly describes the purchasers in a pre-Internet world. Purchasers who, in the main, did as they were advised, took what they were given and came back for more.

The word has a spin-off too: "consumerism". Consumerism is the theory that increasing the consumption of goods is economically beneficial.

Consumerism is a relatively recent concept and is now sometimes deemed to be a pejorative word in that it implies a sophisticated marketing force that impels people to buy both good and bad quality things, whether they need to or not. Consumer groups and consumer activism have emerged as protective forces to counter rampant consumerism.

In fact the word "consumerism" comes into general usage at the time that the affluence of the 1960s puts real disposable income into wallets and purses; income that is targeted by marketers.

There are currently over 96,000 books available on the subject of the consumer. As a descriptor for the person

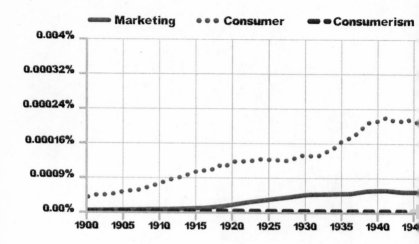

who purchases, it is ingrained into the vocabulary of most marketing people. So much so that it covers not just human physical consumption (of food and drink), but also our usage of services (gas, electricity, bank accounts, etc) and, in fact, of anything we buy.

The principal communication force for marketing to reach consumers has been advertising.

You can only buy a mere 32,000 books on advertising because it has for a long time been a specialist industry, self-regulated and with its own tailor-made processes and training programs.

The term has run into some difficulties now.

For some, advertising is best understood by understanding that the word means what its derivation – ad vertere – intends, ie, "to turn towards (something)".

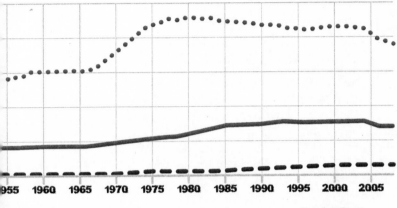

Google NGram

Since 1960 the method for getting someone to turn towards your product was to engage all the media possibilities (particularly TV and newspapers) and employ the arts of surprise, engagement and delight. For a while, these arts elevated some advertising to the status of entertainment in its own right and, indeed, in 1954 a prestigious award ceremony was established in Venice to mimic the Hollywood glamour of the Cannes Film Festival. [50]

For these people, advertising is best understood by only seeing the art of attracting attention to a product or service through a written message, still, or moving picture or both.

For those people it is a craft skill, which cleverly creates

[50] Inspired by the International Film Festival, staged in Cannes since the late 1940s, a group of cinema screen advertising contractors belonging to the Screen Advertising World Association (Sawa) felt the makers of advertising films should be similarly recognized. They established the International Advertising Film Festival, the first of which took place in Venice, Italy, in September 1954, with 187 film entries from 14 countries. The lion of the Piazza San Marco in Venice was the inspiration for the Lion Trophy. The second festival was held in Monte Carlo, and the third in Cannes. After that, the event alternated between Venice and Cannes before settling in the latter in 1984.

an energy when the words and visuals strongly play off each other. For them, this is the world of the TV series Mad Men. It does not embrace today's world of search engine optimization or second-screen technology.

Then there are those for whom the term "advertising" encompasses a wide remit. It embraces any form of commercial communication, both on- and off line. For them, the "Advertising Industry" embraces artists, writers and technicians with equal status and merit.

Advertising has been an important and often dominant market force for over 100 years.

It is a more generally used word by the public than marketing and can often be interchanged with it by those not engaged in either discipline.

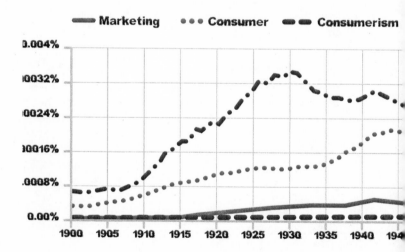

Marketing, consumers, advertising: these seem like easy to grasp notions.

But we are in an implosive environment.

Marketing, consumers and advertising are now completely different concepts. They were creations of a pre-Internet era. A pre-digital era.

They have been subsumed by a much bigger cultural wave.

But they have not died.

The idea that they have died is a common fancy with many "Jeremiah" observers heralding "The Death of Advertising" or "The End of Marketing".

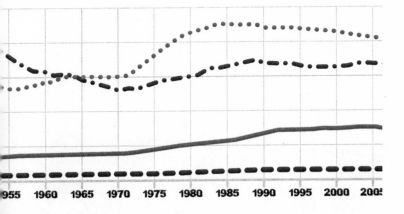

Google NGram

They may have died if they had been superceded by an explosive new invention in the way that the telephone replaced the telegraph and substantially grew the market for connectivity.

But that hasn't happened.

The Web is an innovation, for sure, but it is not one that has changed the things we want to buy. And businesses still need to take their goods to market. We still need to hear about them. It has not changed the need for marketing.

No, the implosive effect of the Internet has done something very, very different to businesses and purchasers.

To explain this let me bring together the summary points of the previous chapters.

We consume the Internet in a way that suggests we can't live without it, even though we never needed it, nor did we ask for it. There's that word again, "consume". But it's used differently. We consume the Internet not as "consumers" but as people in a "needs-based" way.

The Internet is like eating. We do it everyday not because of, but despite, the way businesses want to sell us things.

What else? Well, it has made Homo Sapiens a faster and more flexible animal. It is as if we have a new body part that extends our reach way beyond what we previously thought possible. We no longer see "supply and demand" as an issue. If something is out of stock or not made any more, we can be sure it will appear on eBay at some point. Everything is eventually everywhere.

But the Internet is culturally contrary. It is taking us back into ourselves and exploding inwards the behaviours we already know. It is an implosive force, not an explosive one. This brings excitement of a different kind. Now we are devouring things because we can, not because we need them. We are "re-heating old food" and serving it up in an unexpected way.

We have become our own editors of a kaleidoscopic array of content and now rather than simply enjoy shared experiences we relentlessly pursue the "shareable", with scant regard for its provenance. The shareable "gene" that we have embraced so readily and quickly extends the notion of "word of mouth" into an altogether different stratosphere. This simple statement: "I bought this DVD but the extras were very poor. Wait until the extended version comes out", now has enormous resonance and importance. It can kill or grow a product in one deft individual move.

We are all "screenagers" which means we are much less easily categorized; now businesses need to think less about demographic profiling and more about making individual lives easier to navigate.

Socializing through the Net compounds and compacts offline socializing and drives a regular diet of new tit-bits at an accelerating rate. Socializing is taste driven – that is, individual tastes. Jumping into other people's social media is fine. But if your brand or message is not liked or invited, be prepared to be thrown out as an unwelcome gatecrasher. More importantly, rather than crash other people's lives, it is far better to create your own party that is so attractive that people want to join.

Social media, socializing and socialism do not universally connect. People today operate more in an atomocracy where individuality of needs comes first. An atomocracy has its own unique billions of social mores and culture-defining snapshots of what's in and what's out. An atomocracy is you and your screen, your network and your likes/dislikes. It's a dangerous place for salesmen!

Finally, we are all in the same boat. Companies and customers alike are consuming the Internet together. The screen is the same doorway for companies, competitors and customers. Companies need to build-in desirability for a product or service at the invention and tooling stage. Then, like Amazon, they must focus on the process of delivery.

And this is the point.

To do this companies must be digital themselves.

Look at how "digital" has entered our language.

Digital (ie, our relationship with, and behaviour towards, the many access points in and out of the Internet) is the water in which we now all swim.

A company must be digital, behave digitally and be organized digitally in order to use, and benefit from, digitized media and our new need for Internet consumption. As we saw earlier, five years ago, 50% of all global media was digital. By 2020 that ratio will be 80%.

So it is no surprise that marketing is now a major driver of IT purchases. In fact Gartner, the research firm, predicts that by 2017, Chief Marketing Officers will buy more technology for their companies than Chief Information Officers.[51]

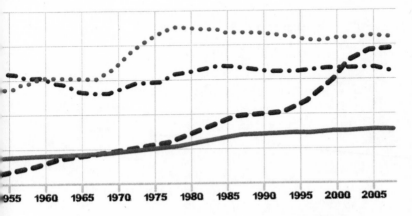

Digital

1955 1960 1965 1970 1975 1980 1985 1990 1995 2000 2005

Google NGram

[51] http://my.gartner.com/portal/server.pt?open=512&objID=202&mode=2&PageID=5553&resId=1871515&ref=Webinar-Calendar

This is somewhat of a renaissance of marketing, which, as mentioned, has been regularly written off over the past 20 years.

But this new "digital marketing" needs to understand that it cannot operate as a siloed function. "Digital" does not equate to "silo".

The remainder of the business cannot devolve the responsibility for "Being Digital" to the marketing department.

Businesses must BE digital, not just DO digital.

More importantly, businesses need to understand how the Internet has changed them.

You might say, "Company, Know Thyself".

It has changed the way companies are viewed and used.

It has changed the way products and services are priced and delivered.

It has changed the way businesses must relate to customers.

Opposite is one of the communication models we use at our business consultancy Fearlessly Frank. It is a simple, straightforward schema showing the key stages of commercial communication from the 1950s to today.

Importantly, all four stages are operating simultaneously. We have not lost the monologue communication of the 1950s (think about paid-for party political messaging and, still, a lot of advertising).

Media Organization of the Modern World

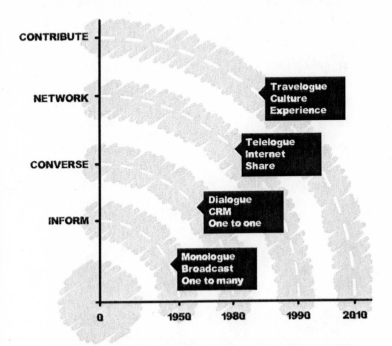

Customer Relationship Management has moved from paper (leaflet)-based direct marketing through to a sophisticated software process and it lives happily alongside, and regularly works with, the Internet.

"Telelogical" communication is my expression for communication that comes from the farthest possible points on the planet. It is the widespread many-to-many communication enabled by the Internet and, more specifically, social network and crowd source sites.

Finally, "travelogue" is my expression for how modern communication – whether it be businesses to customer, or purely inter-personal – must work. Importantly it infers that companies must run in parallel with their customers, going to the places they are going to, at the same time and in the same way.

Communication has to be as natural and enjoyable as a conversation with a stranger in, say, a railway carriage. Companies must contribute to customers' lives by making the process of interaction simplicity itself. That means the process must be fluid, fast and effortless. Companies, brands, services, products and customers are all atomocracies of equal standing communicating to each other.

The exciting aspect to this is that, given confluence and consistency of behaviour, each atomocracy can be equally accepted onto each others' journey. Companies now have the capability to sit with customers, not sell to them.

The model suggests that we have moved beyond a networked society and into a multi-contributory world. It's not enough to say that we share things. Our habitual, natural everyday behaviour edits, alters and deletes what we share so that we each, in our individual atomocracies, become net contributors to our own communities of what we determine to be "shareable".

The model also shows how the Internet now has the potential to move us from being recipients of a medium to active agents harnessing a new physiological necessity. The medium of communication today is one of a changed cultural landscape, containing all players at the same time whether they are buyers or sellers. This essentially is the ultimate expression of being digital.

Our consumption of the Internet is mainly free. Yes, we buy a broadband data package for home and mobile, but a large proportion of time spent on the Internet is transacting for free, by ourselves. This feels less like a commercial environment and more like a natural one.

In a natural environment you would expect a more natural transaction process. Amazon, for example, achieves this and remains the model for online retailing. When we buy from Amazon we do not expect a "personal service", we expect a "process service" as natural as a walk on the beach (with or without other people).

When the "Internet of Things", or "The Internet of Everything" connects so much of our material lives and transmits their value in bits, we expect that transmission to be fluid.

Humans are now an integral part of the fluid processes.

For companies this is important.

There is a New Order, created by implosive effects.

We are all no longer consumers. In fact, we are no longer customers. Yes we make purchase decisions. But these decisions are like editing a programme schedule.

Whilst the Internet often feels free, we all know it isn't. We pay for it with the detail of our lives because it is now a natural function of our lives. We are, in fact, all processors. We have evolved to be active agents in the world of commercial transactions. We are not passive purchasers.

Importantly, we are communicators in our networks.

Companies must recognize this and buy our time and attention as if they were booking a seat next to us on a train and taking a journey with us. We decide whether to attend to the company's conversation and, if we do, we will almost certainly edit, add or delete information just as any other channel providing content would do.

Products and services are now the transactions of companies using our own personal media. If we choose to take the transaction on board we may, or may not, choose to transmit that to some of our entire network.

If the Internet had behaved like every other preceding invention, we should all be discovering unimagined places.

We aren't.

Instead we have become unimagined people.

And this is when the fun begins.

Our unimagined lives will increasingly coalesce around our own personal networks, as well as our social networks.

We will be able to manage these personal networks initially through the existing basic aggregator sites such as Groupon, MultiMe and ifttt.

It is the natural reaction to what has been a very unnatural existence.

The Internet implosion has created a difference between Personal (lower) and Internet (higher) pressure. This higher pressure, outside our lives, has been so large and intense that the structure of our analogue lives has collapsed inward into itself.

But implosions come to a conclusion.

We are soon to experience (maybe we are right now) the moment at which the Internet will detonate an explosive force. This explosion should eventually lead to a new period of "enlightenment" where everything from how we move, interact and behave (think transport, currency, commerce, healthcare, community, education, reproduction, sex, recreation, religion) may well resemble something that is totally unrecognizable today.

At the point of elaborate personal online integration, the implosive force will create a society of self-controlled personal media, or "transactional", assets.

We will be able to use the power of our own edited purchasing patterns to demand more and more from businesses. We are already beginning to do this, as the success of Groupon demonstrates.

But we will go much much further. We, in essence, will create a personalized world which will more naturally coalesce around like-minded others. Think of it as "super-connected selves", whereby our reach out to greater personal advancement will be extended and magnified by automatic aggregation.

The concomitant purchasing and bargaining power will be immense, but more importantly the push for newer products and services will come thick and fast.

Those companies that are fluid and flexible enough to feed and contribute to this new "explosion of desire" will be survivors in what will inevitably be a fight for the perfect digital fit.

About the Author

Andy Law is widely recognized as one of the world's foremost practitioners of breakthrough business thinking. He is currently Chairman of Fearlessly Frank and was previously CEO of Chiat/Day London and founder of St. Lukes' worldwide group of advertising agencies. He is the author of *Open Minds* (*Creative Company* in the USA) and *Experiment at Work* and a regular blogger for *The Huffington Post*.

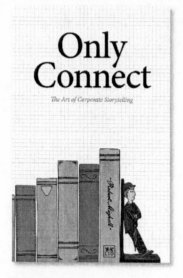

ISBN: 9781907794452

A coherent story can make you better understood, believed in and trusted. So why is the business world only just discovering its power? This book draws on the psychology, history, and of course, the greatest works, of storytelling to show how modern businesses can communicate more effectively and creatively.

Robert Mighall explains why story has a universal power to move people. He shows how to build a compelling core story, and apply that across a range of communications. And he demonstrates how trends in social media and content marketing are making this most ancient communication art ever more urgently relevant. What the corporate world needs most, story does best: establish the human connections upon which trust is build. And this book explains how.

ALSO PUBLISHED BY LID PUBLISHING:

The making of Dirt is Good
A personal journey of
Brand Transformation

David Arkwright
Former Global VP Persil and Omo, Unilever
Founder of MEAT Global Brand Consultancy

ISBN: 9781907794469

In 2005, Unilever ignored whiter than white in favour of mud and grease and launched its "Dirt is Good" marketing campaign, for its Persil and OMO washing detergents. The campaign was devised by David Arkwright and his marketing team in Unilever.

Today, it continues to be one of Unilver's most successful campaigns. As well as transforming the Persil and OMO brands, the campaign has become a defining moment in the whole marketing and branding world. This book, written by the person at the helm of "Dirt is Good", is an essential case study in creating a global brand with an idea at its very core. The book reveals the trials, challenges and successes experienced by Arkwright and his team, told in a very personal and engaging real-time adventure. And for marketers today, the book includes real and practical learnings from this ground-breaking campaign.

ALSO PUBLISHED BY LID PUBLISHING:

ISBN: 9781907794124

"A valuable piece of thinking making a valuable piece of reading."
Daniel Finkelstein, Executive Editor, *Times*

"A stimulating and concise read, insightful and pragmatic."
Director magazine.

"This book offers a wealth of advice on how individuals can learn to lead through the `noise' and successfully challenge the status quo."
European CEO magazine.

Challenger organizations are those companies which are disrupting their market and taking serious market share from their competitors. Such companies typically have an ambition beyond the conventional resources available to them. They are innovative and radical, and most enjoy significant and sustained periods of growth.

This book analyses the practices and disciplines that underpin the successful Challenger organization. In particular, it looks at how Challenger leadership and culture can be developed in large, complex, established organizations.

BEYOND
THE WRITTEN WORD

Authors who speak to you face to face.

Discover LID Speakers, a service that enables businesses to have direct and interactive contact with the best ideas brought to their own sector by the most outstanding creators of business thinking.

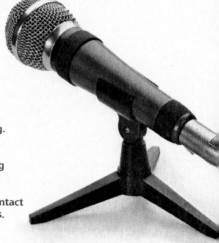

- A network specialising in business speakers, making it easy to find the most suitable candidates.

- A website with full details and videos, so you know exactly who you're hiring.

- A forum packed with ideas and suggestions about the most interesting and cutting-edge issues.

- A place where you can make direct contact with the best in international speakers.

- The only speakers' bureau backed up by the expertise of an established business book publisher.

LIDspeakers
.com

Sure value.